...ta

...OK

...hour

...SON
...ice
...Hall

• Toronto
...lew Delhi
...ris • Milan

LIB (c)

Pearson Education Limited
Edinburgh Gate
Harlow CM20 2JE
Tel: +44 (0)1279 623623
Fax: +44 (0)1279 431059
Website: www.pearsoned.co.uk

First published in Great Britain in 2007

@ Jerri Ledford 2007

The rights of Jerri Ledford and Rebecca Freshour to be identified as authors of this work have been asserted by them in accordance with the Copyright, Designs and Patents Act 1988.

ISBN: 978-0-132-34060-1

British Library Cataloguing-in-Publication Data
A catalogue record for this book is available from the British Library

10 9 8 7 6 5 4 3 2 1
11 10 09 08 07

Typeset in 10pt Helvetica by 3
Printed and bound in Great Britain by Ashford Colour Press Ltd., Gosport

The publisher's policy is to use paper manufactured from sustainable forests.

Brilliant Pocket Books

What you need to know – when you need it!

When you're working on your PC and come up against a problem that you're unsure how to solve, or want to accomplish something in an application that you aren't sure how to do, where do you look? If you are fed up with wading through pages of background information in unwieldy manuals and training guides trying to find the piece of information or advice that you need RIGHT NOW, and if you find that helplines really aren't that helpful, then Brilliant Pocket Books are the answer!

Brilliant Pocket Books have been developed to allow you to find the info that you need easily and without fuss and to guide you through each task using a highly visual step-by-step approach – providing exactly what you need to know, when you need it!

Brilliant Pocket Books are concise, easy-to-access guides to all of the most common, important and useful tasks in all of the applications in the Office 2007 suite. Short, concise lessons make it really easy to learn any particular feature, or master any task or problem that you will come across in day-to-day use of the applications.

When you are faced with any task on your PC, whether major or minor, that you are unsure about, your Brilliant Pocket Book will provide you with the answer – almost before you know what the question is!

Brilliant Pocket Books Series

Series Editor: Joli Ballew

Brilliant Microsoft® Access 2007 Pocket Book *S.E. Slack*

Brilliant Microsoft® Excel 2007 Pocket Book *J. Peter Bruzzese*

Brilliant Microsoft® Office 2007 Pocket Book *Jerri Ledford & Rebecca Freshour*

Brilliant Microsoft® Outlook 2007 Pocket Book *Meryl K. Evans*

Brilliant Microsoft® PowerPoint 2007 Pocket Book *S.E. Slack*

Brilliant Microsoft® Windows Vista Pocket Book *Jerri Ledford & Rebecca Freshour*

Brilliant Microsoft® Word 2007 Pocket Book *Deanna Reynolds*

Contents

Introduction

Welcome to the *Brilliant Microsoft® Windows Vista Pocket Book* – a handy visual quick reference that will give you a basic grounding in the common features and tasks that you will need to master to use Microsoft® Windows Vista in any day-to-day situation. Keep it on your desk, in your briefcase or bag – or even in your pocket! – and you will always have the answer to hand for any problem or task that you come across.

Find out what you need to know – when you need it!

You don't have to read this book in any particular order. It is designed so that you can jump in, get the information you need and jump out – just look up the task in the contents list, turn to the right page, read the introduction, follow the step-by-step instructions – and you're done!

How this book works

Each section in this book includes foolproof step-by-step instructions for performing specific tasks, using screenshots to illustrate each step. Additional information is included to help increase your understanding and develop your skills – these are identified by the following icons:

Jargon buster – New or unfamiliar terms are defined and explained in plain English to help you as you work through a section.

Timesaver tip – These tips give you ideas that cut corners and confusion. They also give you additional information related to the topic that you are currently learning. Use them to expand your knowledge of a particular feature or concept.

Important – This identifies areas where new users often run into trouble, and offers practical hints and solutions to these problems.

Brilliant Pocket Books **are a handy, accessible resource that you will find yourself turning to time and time again when you are faced with a problem or an unfamiliar task and need an answer at your fingertips – or in your pocket!**

1

Getting Started in Windows Vista

In this lesson you'll find out what's new in Windows Vista, how to install it and how to get help and support.

→ What's New in Windows Vista?

With its new and enhanced features and the very user-friendly desktop, Windows Vista is sure to become the favourite operating system from Microsoft. This operating system offers an improved user experience with features such as a new start menu, improved folders and live icons.

Microsoft Windows Vista offers many new features, including Windows Aero, which provides a cleaner, transparent look and wonderful graphic quality, plus live icons and a Windows Flip 3D feature (though this is not available on all versions); a sidebar on the desktop that displays mini-applications, called gadgets, that allow access to features such as a clock, calendar and currency exchange; and Windows Search, which allows you to search for files and applications anywhere on your computer.

Jargon buster

Gadgets are small applications that can be added to or removed from your Windows Desktop with a few clicks of your mouse. On the release of Vista, more than 100 gadgets were available, but that number climbs steadily as developers continue to create new gadgets.

Microsoft also offers better security in Vista than was the case in previous operating systems. For example, Vista features more advanced parental controls, two different firewalls and a new security feature called User Account Control (UAC).

→ Installing Windows Vista

If you're upgrading to Windows Vista, you will need to install the operating system over your current operating system. Most new computers are available with Vista pre-installed.

Important

It is not at all uncommon to find that brand new computers include Office Vista but do not meet the minimum requirements of the operating system. Computer manufacturers sell computers this way to increase their upgrade sales. Check any new computer that you're considering closely to ensure that, at the very least, the minimum resource requirements for Vista are met.

Installation Requirements

To ensure that Windows Vista operates at maximum efficiency, you should make sure that your computer meets the system requirements for the operating system.

The minimum system requirements to run the Microsoft Windows Vista operating system (as recommended by Microsoft) are a 1 GHz 32-bit or 64-bit processor, 1 GB of RAM and at least a 40 GB hard drive with 15 GB of free hard disk space. Keep in mind that the faster your processor, the larger your hard drive and the more RAM you have, the better will be the performance of any operating system.

Important

Although the minimum requirements for Microsoft Vista include 1 GB of RAM, it's best to operate your computer with at least 2 GB of RAM in order for Vista to be at its most efficient. Additionally, you should ensure that the video card included in your computer meets the stiff requirements of Vista.

There are a few additional requirements that need to be met before you install Microsoft Windows Vista. These include a DVD-ROM drive, mouse or some other pointing device, keyboard and a graphics processing unit (GPU). The GPU should be

Direct X 9 capable and support a WDDM driver, have Pixel
Shader 2.0 in the hardware and have 32 bits per pixel capability.

Installation Instructions

Once you are sure that you have the correct system
requirements to operate Windows Vista, then you can install the
operating system. Take the following steps before you begin
installation to ensure that it is a stress-free process.

- Be sure to back up your data before upgrading to Windows
  Vista. If everything goes smoothly, the upgrade should not
  affect your data, but it's always wise to do a complete backup
  before installing any software on your computer just in case.

- Perform a routine virus scan, correct any problems that are
  found and then disable your virus protection program.
  Antivirus programs can interfere with the Windows Vista
  installation process, so be sure to do all of this prior to
  installation.

- Shut down any programs that you may have been using
  before you begin the installation and be sure to disconnect
  from the Internet. These actions simply ensure that nothing
  interferes with your installation process.

Now you can follow the steps below for installing Microsoft
Windows Vista.

1 Insert the Microsoft Windows Vista installation disk into your
DVD or CD drive.

2 An **Install Windows dialogue box** appears. Click on **Install
Now**.

3 A page appears prompting you to get important updates
before you begin the installation process. Choose to complete
these updates as they will help your computer to operate
more efficiently once the installation has been completed.

4 Next, you are prompted to enter your **product key** for
authentication. This is the 25-character product key that is

found on a sticker on the back of your Microsoft Windows
Vista CD jewel case. Type in these digits carefully as they
must appear on your screen exactly as they appear on the
jewel case or the software cannot be authenticated.

5 On the next installation page you must choose to accept the
terms of the licence. Be sure to read the licence agreement
completely, then click on **Continue**. If you do not accept the
licensing terms you will not be able to install Microsoft
Windows Vista on your computer.

6 Next, you are prompted to choose the type of installation
you would like to perform – either an upgrade or a new
installation. Make the correct selection, and the operating
system will be installed on your computer. Expect the
computer to reboot several times during this process.

7 Once the installation has been completed, you must turn
your computer off completely. Leave it off for about 30
seconds, then you can turn it back on. Doing this helps to
ensure that your new operating system will start correctly.

Registering Vista

Once you have installed Microsoft Windows Vista on your
computer, you will automatically be prompted to register Vista
with Microsoft. To do this you must either be connected to the
Internet (the quickest route) or call an 0800 number. If you skip the
registration process, you'll be prompted to register the software
each time that you start your computer until you have done so.

→ Finding Help and Support in Vista

Finding help and support in Vista is easier than it has ever been
with any other operating system. There are two ways to access
help and support. One method is to click on **Start** and select
Help and Support, located on the right side of the menu.

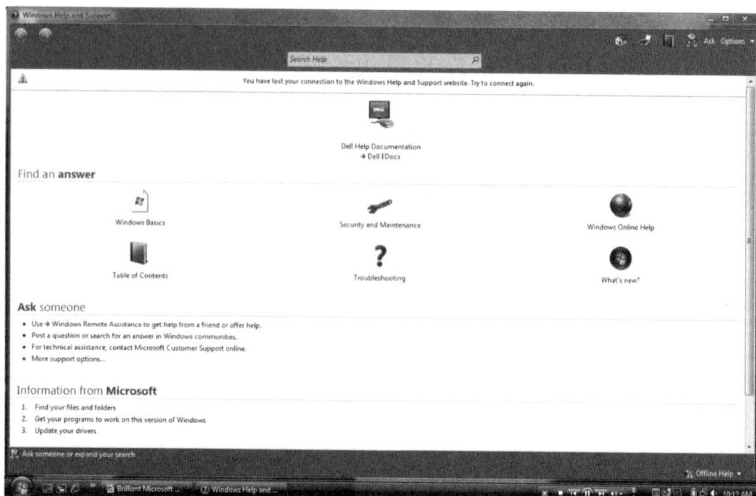

Figure 1.1
Help and Support menu.

In the **Help and Support** dialogue box that appears, select any of the icons that are shown or type your question directly into the Search Help box (as seen in Figure 1.1). Vista will search the help files on your computer and online to find you an answer.

Another way to access help and support is to type your search parameters in the white box on your taskbar.

→ Accessing Vista

To access Vista, turn your computer on. As Microsoft Windows Vista is now your operating system, it will automatically run when the computer boots up.

→ Familiarising Yourself with the Desktop

In Vista, the appearance of the desktop has changed, as has the layout of the menus, and new features are also available. One

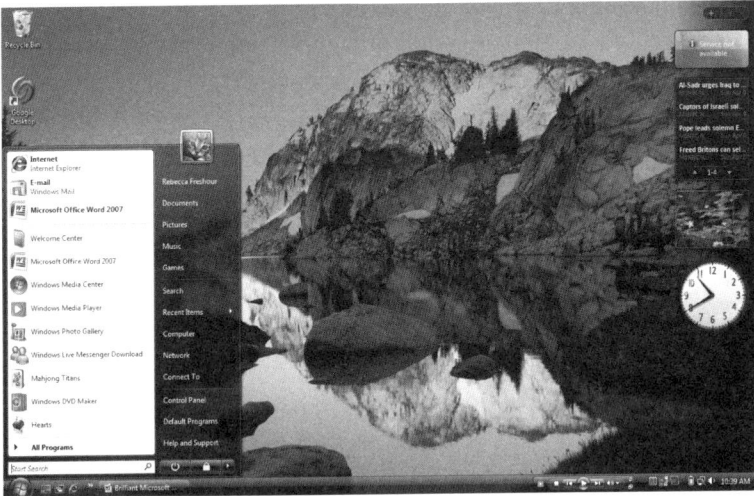

Figure 1.2
New start menu view.

new feature of the Vista desktop is the sidebar, which allows you to customise the gadgets that will increase your daily work flow. For example, you can add a calculator and a file transfer protocol (FTP) gadget to your sidebar so that you don't have to search for these tools each time you need them. You also now have search options in your taskbar at the bottom of your desktop.

Accessing the Start Menu

The start menu in Vista looks a little different from that of previous operating systems. Instead of the start button that you're accustomed to seeing at the bottom of the desktop, there is now a Windows button. You'll find it in the bottom left corner of the desktop, as shown in Figure 1.2. Click on the **Windows button** and the **start menu** appears. The start menu has been redesigned for Windows Vista to allow easier access to programs, documents and common components of Windows.

Using the Taskbar

The taskbar is located at the bottom of the Windows Vista desktop. It contains your **start menu** on the far left and your notification area to the far right. The notification area contains a clock, volume control icon and additional icons that represent the software that is installed on your computer. The icons will vary from one computer to another depending on what programs the user has installed or removed. You can find out what any icon is for by holding your pointer over it for about a second.

You can use your tray icons to access certain settings of your programs. For example, if you right-click on the clock, you can choose to adjust the time. A dialogue box appears in which you make such adjustments and, when you've finished, click on **Save.**

Your taskbar also has a search box to the left of your notification area. By typing a word or phrase to look for (for example, Help and Support), Windows will search your hard drive and then show the search results as links that you can click on to go to that information.

The area between your start menu icon and your notification area will show you what programs you currently have open. By clicking on any of these boxes, you can minimise or maximise that program. You can also right-click on the boxes to restore or close these programs.

Figure 1.3
The recycle bin icon.

Managing the Recycle Bin

The only primary icon that Windows Vista provides you with on
the desktop is the recycle bin icon, as shown in Figure 1.3. This
is where you put your "rubbish". You can remove or delete files
that you no longer need, icons on your desktop you don't wish to
have there or any other items that you have finished with by
dragging each one on the recycle bin icon.

Important

You should never just delete programs. Instead, go to **Control Panel >
Add/Remove Programs** and highlight the program that you would like
to remove in the list that appears. Next, click on **Remove** and follow
any additional prompts made by the system. Removing programs
using this method ensures files that might affect other programs aren't
accidentally deleted.

The good news about the recycle bin is that, unless it's a file from
a network drive or removable storage drive, once you have sent it
to the recycle bin, it is still recoverable. This comes in handy if
you happen to send something to the recycle bin that you later
find you still need. To restore something that you have sent to the
recycle bin, double-click on the recycle bin icon and, when it
opens, find the object or document that you would like to restore.
Right-click on that icon and then click on **Restore**. That item is
returned to its original location on your hard drive. Keep in mind
that if the recycle bin becomes full, it will start self-deleting the
oldest items in the bin and those items will not be recoverable.

When the recycle bin is open, you will see a view that is very
different from what you have seen in the past. There are two new
items in the dropdown menu. These are the Views menu, which
allows you to choose the size and presentation of your icons and
view a detailed listing of the item's original location and the date
that it was moved to the recycle bin, as Figure 1.4 shows.

Figure 1.4
The recycle bin.

In the Views menu you also have the "Empty the Recycle Bin"
command, as shown in Figure 1.5, and the "Restore all items"
icon. When you select the Empty the Recycle Bin icon, everything
in the recycle bin is permanently deleted, so make sure that you
really want to delete it before you select this option.

Figure 1.5
The "Empty Recycle Bin" icon.

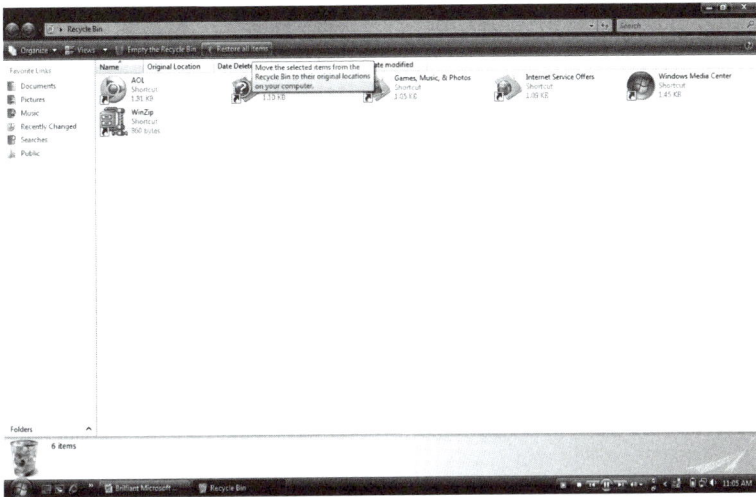

Figure 1.6
The "Restore all items" icon.

Clicking on the "Restore all items" icon, as shown in Figure 1.6, will restore all of the files and documents currently in the recycle bin to their original locations on your hard drive.

2

Customising Vista

In this lesson you'll learn about customising the Start Menu, Taskbar and display as well as working with the Windows Sidebar.

→ Customising the Start Menu

The first thing you have probably noticed about Vista is that it looks very different from previous versions of Microsoft operating systems. In addition to looking different, however, you also have some additional customisation capabilities. You can begin your customisation with the start menu.

To customise your start menu, follow these steps.

1 Click on the **Windows button** to open the **start menu**, then select **Control Panel** from the right side of the start menu.

2 When the **control panel dialogue box** appears, select **Appearance and Personalization**, as shown in Figure 2.1.

3 In the **Appearance and Personalization dialogue box**, select **Taskbar and Start Menu**.

4 Click on **Customize the Start menu**.

5 The **Taskbar and Start Menu Properties** dialogue box opens to the **Start Menu tab**. Select the **Start menu type** to

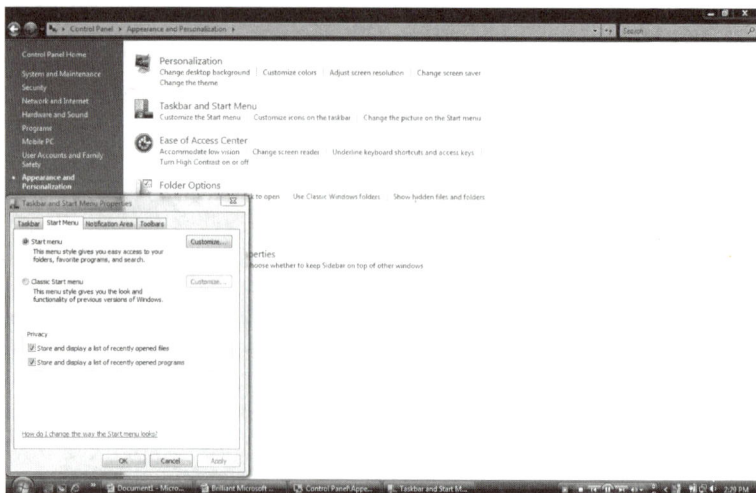

Figure 2.1
Start menu properties.

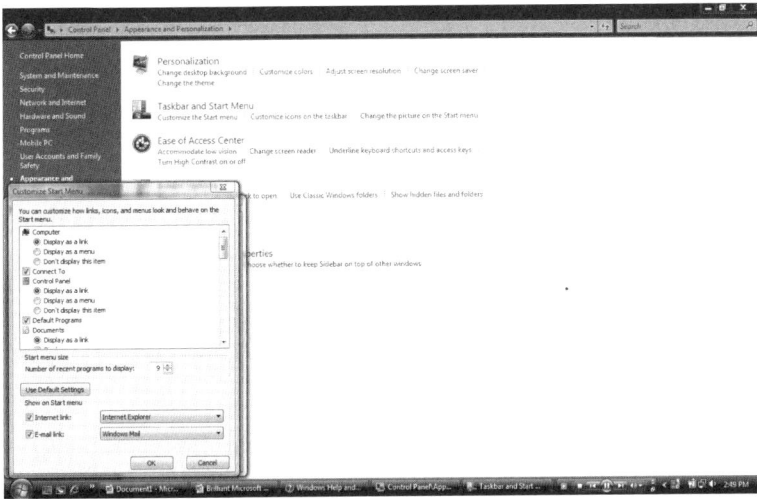

Figure 2.2
Start menu settings.

customise. You can choose to use the default Vista start
menu or step back to a menu that resembles the previous
version of the Microsoft operating system.

6 Next, click on **Customize.** The **Customize Start Menu**
dialogue box shown in Figure 2.2 appears. Select the
customisation that you would like to apply to the start menu
and then click on **OK**. You will be returned to the taskbars
and **Start Menu Properties dialogue box**.

Customisation options that you have for the start menu include
the following.

■ **Choose program options**—This is the main menu in the
customisation pane. Click on the button beside an option to
select or deselect that option.

■ **Start menu size**—Vista will display programs that were
opened recently as an attempt to help the user work more
efficiently. Increasing or decreasing the start menu size (by
number) will determine the number of recently used programs

displayed in the start menu. You can choose to view up to 30 recently used programs.

■ **Show on start menu**—This allows you to set the programs that you would like to use for Internet and e-mail applications. To select a program other than the default, open the dropdown menu and select the program that you want to use. Alternatively, the options can be deselected if you do not wish them to be displayed at all.

If you make changes to the start menu that you do not like, you can return to the original settings by clicking on **Use Default Settings**.

When you have finished customising your start menu, click on **Apply** and then click on **OK** to save your settings.

→ Creating Shortcuts

Shortcuts allow you to display icons of frequently used files and programs on your desktop to keep you from ploughing through the start menu and all programs to access applications that you are working in. If there are unwanted shortcuts on your desktop, you can delete them without deleting the whole program. Just right-click on the icon and select **Delete** from the menu that appears. You will be prompted to confirm your decision.

To add a shortcut to your desktop, take the following steps.

1 Select the **start menu**.

2 Click on **All Programs** and locate the program or file for which you would like to create a shortcut.

3 Right-click on that program and then, in the menu that appears (shown in Figure 2.3), select **Send To > Desktop (create shortcut)**. The icon for that program then appears on the desktop.

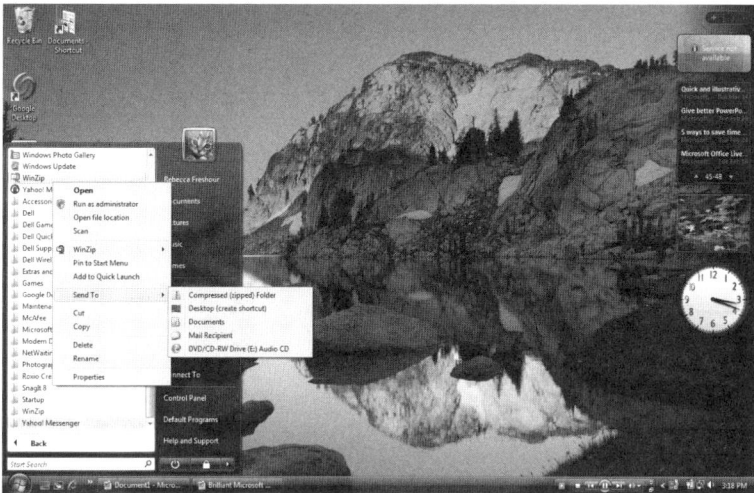

Figure 2.3
Program menu for shortcut.

To delete a shortcut from your desktop, right-click on the
shortcut icon and select **Delete** or click on and drag the icon to
your recycling bin.

→ Customising the Taskbar

Customising your taskbar allows you to change the way it
appears, as well as how it acts.

To customise your taskbar follow these steps.

1 Click on the **start button**.

2 Select **Control Panel**.

3 Select **Appearance and Personalization**.

4 Select **Customize icons on the taskbar**.

5 In the **Taskbar and Start Menu Properties dialogue
   box** that appears, select the **Taskbar** tab, as shown in
   Figure 2.4.

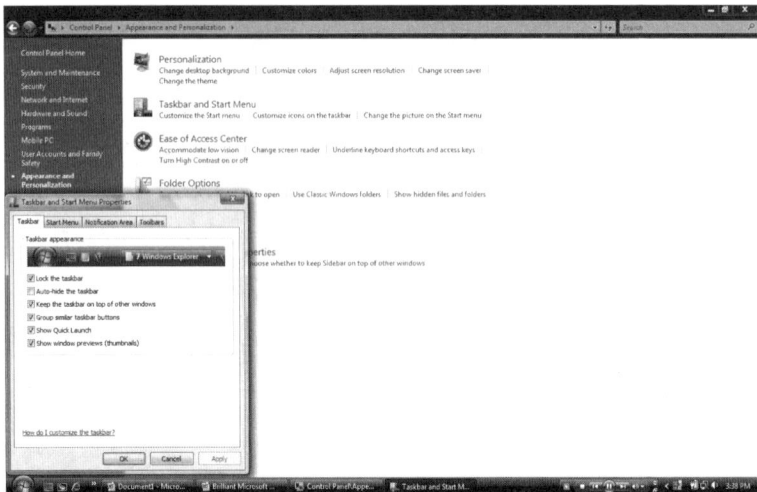

Figure 2.4
Taskbar tab.

6 Place ticks next to the desired options by clicking on the boxes and then click on **Apply.** There are six modifications to choose from:

- **Lock the taskbar**—If you lock the taskbar, the size cannot be changed and it cannot be moved to any other position on the desktop.

- **Auto-hide the taskbar**—This setting hides the taskbar when it is not in use. To view the taskbar in this mode, point the mouse to the location of the taskbar and it reappears.

- **Keep the taskbar on top of other windows**—This setting keeps the taskbar on top of any window in which you are working.

- **Group similar taskbar buttons**—This setting keeps similar programs and files that are open together on the taskbar. For example, if you have two Word documents open, they will be side by side in the taskbar. If too many programs or files are open, it will put the similar ones into a pop-up menu.

- **Show Quick Launch**—Here you can access often-used programs by clicking their icons on the taskbar.

- **Show window previews (thumbnails)**—Allows you to preview the files that are open in your taskbar by viewing a thumbnail of the file.

Timesaver tip

A faster way to get to the taskbar tab is to right-click on an empty area of the taskbar, click on **Properties**, then click on the **Taskbar tab**.

In addition to the taskbar items, you can customise what you would like to see in the notification area of your taskbar (on the far right side) by selecting the **Notification Area tab** (see Figure 2.5). Select and deselect the items that you want to appear on the taskbar and then select **Apply**. When you've finished, click on **OK** to close the dialogue box.

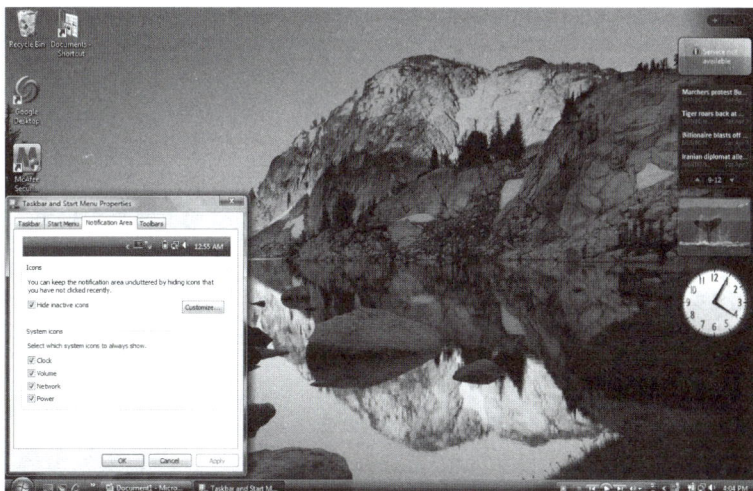

Figure 2.5
Notification area tab.

→ Customising Your Display

You can customise your display by changing the display settings, colour and appearance, setting the background, selecting a screensaver or selecting custom sounds.

Changing Display Settings

To change your display settings, follow these steps.

1 Right-click on an empty area on your desktop.

2 From the menu that appears, select **Personalize**.

3 Select **Display Settings** from the **Personalization dialogue box**.

4 As shown in Figure 2.6, the **Display Settings dialogue box** appears.

5 Make your selections and then click on **Apply**.

6 Click on **OK** to close the dialogue box and return to the **Personalization menu**.

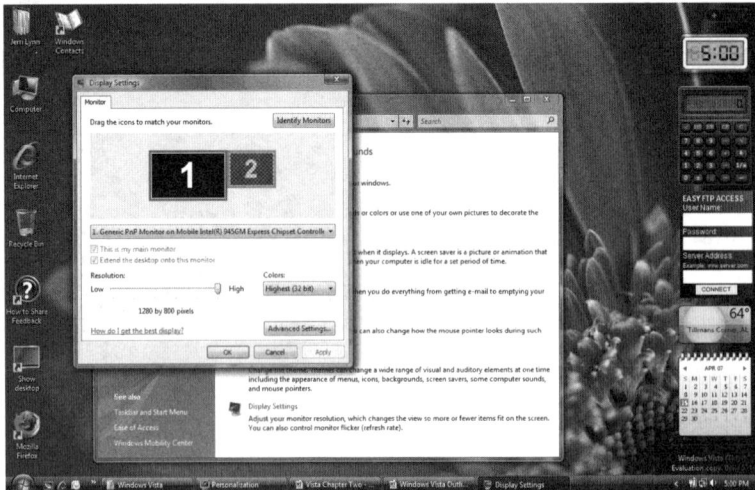

Figure 2.6
Use the Display Settings dialogue box to adjust your display settings.

Important

In the **Display Settings dialogue box**, there is a button that leads you to advanced options. These options are more technical and cover issues such as adapters, monitors and colour management. It is recommended that you do not change any of these settings unless you are very familiar with how they will affect your computer.

Changing Colour and Appearance

To change the colour and appearance of your desktop, take the following steps.

1 Right-click on an empty area on your desktop.

2 From the menu that appears, select **Personalize.**

3 Select **Window Color and Appearance.** The **Window Color and Appearance dialogue box** appears, as shown in Figure 2.7.

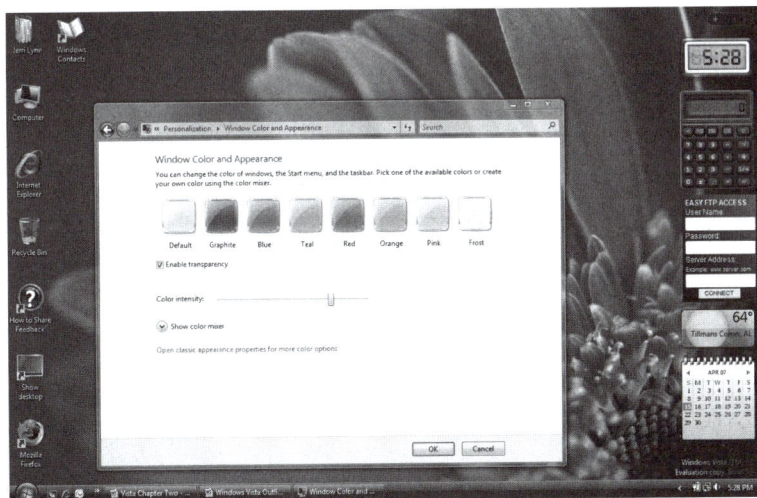

Figure 2.7
Use the Window Color and Appearance dialogue box to adjust how your desktop looks.

4 Select the colour you would like to apply from those shown.

5 Next, select or deselect **Enable transparency**. This option allows you to see through the borders around open windows.

6 Use the slider to adjust the colour intensity of the borders around windows. There is also the option **Show Color Mixer**, which allows you to more precisely adjust the colour you have chosen.

7 When you've finished making your selections, click on **OK** and you will be returned to the **Personalization dialogue box**.

Setting Your Background

To set the background for your desktop, do the following.

1 Right-click on an empty area on your desktop.

2 From the menu that appears, select **Personalize.**

3 Select **Desktop Background**. The **Desktop Background dialogue box** – shown in Figure 2.8 – opens.

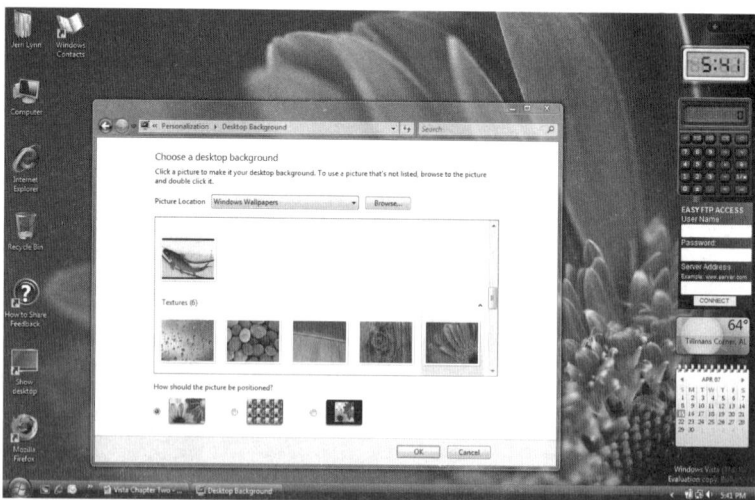

Figure 2.8
Use the Desktop Background dialogue box to change the appearance of your desktop.

4 Select the **Picture Location dropdown menu** and choose the location of the picture (or solid colour) that you would like to apply to your desktop. If you prefer to use a picture that you have in another location on your computer, click on the **Browse button** and navigate to that file.

5 Select the background that you would like to use from the thumbnails that appear before the **Picture Location menu**.

6 Then choose how the picture should be positioned.

7 When you've finished making your selections, click on **OK** and you will be returned to the **Personalization dialogue box**.

Selecting a Screensaver

Screensavers were once a way to extend the life of your computer monitor – also called a screen. Today, monitors are much more durable than they were in the past, but screensavers are still popular. To apply a screensaver to your desktop follow these steps.

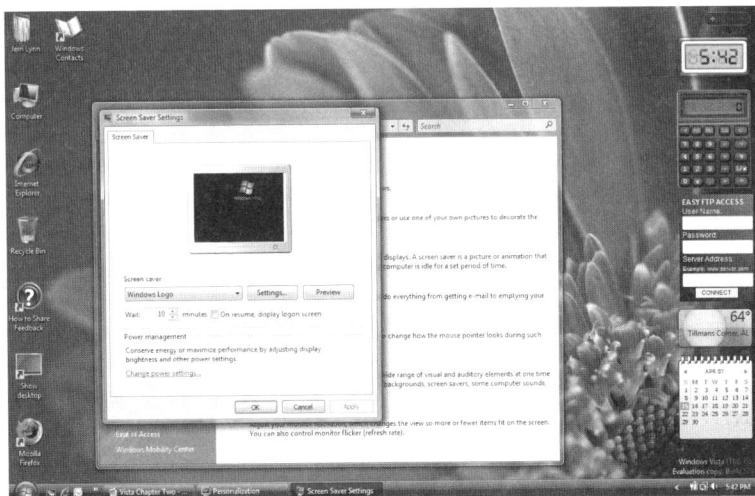

Figure 2.9
The Screen Saver dialogue box allows you to set up a screensaver.

1 Right-click on an empty area on your desktop.

2 From the menu that appears, select **Personalize.**

3 Select **Screen Saver settings**. The **Screen Saver settings dialogue box** appears, as shown in Figure 2.9.

4 In the **Screen Saver** section of the dialogue box, select the dropdown menu to choose the screensaver that you would like to apply. If you don't want a screensaver, then make sure that **(None)** is selected.

5 Next, click on **Settings**. If the screensaver you have selected has additional options that can be set, then you'll be taken to the **Settings dialogue box**. If there are no additional settings, a message will display that says **No Options**.

6 If you would like to preview what your selected screensaver will look like, click on the **Preview button**.

7 You may also set the length of time your computer must be inactive for before the screensaver clicks in (this is to be found below the screensaver dropdown menu).

8 When you have finished choosing your settings, click on **Apply** and then **OK** to return to the **Personalization dialogue box**.

Using Custom Sounds

Customising your sounds is easy. Follow these steps.

1 Right-click on an empty area on your desktop.

2 From the menu that appears, select **Personalize.**

3 In the **Personalize dialogue box**, select **Sounds.** The **Sounds dialogue box** appears, as shown in Figure 2.10.

4 The **Sounds** tab should be selected by default. If it is not, select it.

5 From the **Sound Scheme dropdown menu**, select the sound scheme that you would like to use. Unless you have

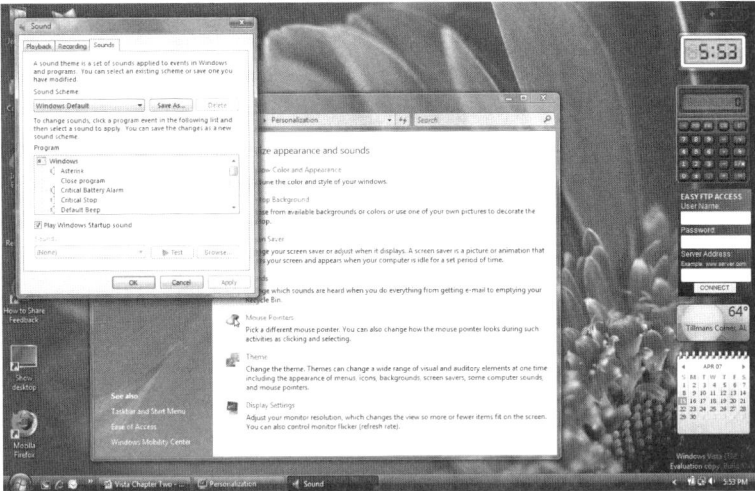

Figure 2.10
Use the Sounds dialogue box to customise your sound settings.

installed a sound scheme that you have downloaded to your computer, your options here will only be **Windows Default** and **No Sounds.**

6 In the **Program area** of the **Sounds dialogue box**, there is a list of sounds available for certain actions that you carry out on your computer. To change the sound for one of those actions, click on the action and then select the **Sounds dropdown menu** below it to choose a different sound. If the sound you want to apply is not listed there, you can select **Browse** and locate the file on your hard drive.

7 If you would like to preview the sound before you commit to it, click on the **Test button** to play the sound.

8 When you have finished making your selections, click on **Apply** and then click on **OK** to return to the **Personalization dialogue box**.

9 If you choose not to make changes to your sound scheme, you can click on the **Cancel button** and any changes that you made will be discarded, then you'll be returned to the **Personalization menu**.

Changing Your Mouse Pointer

Some people find that the pointer is difficult for them to locate and others just prefer to have a fun pointer. To customise your pointer, follow these steps.

1 Right-click on an empty area on your desktop.

2 From the menu that appears, select **Personalize.**

3 From the **Personalization dialogue box**, select **Mouse Pointers**. The **Mouse Properties dialogue box** appears, as shown in Figure 2.11.

4 In the **Scheme section** of the dialogue box, choose the new pointer that you want to use. The pointers in the **Customize section** will change to reflect their appearance with the pointer that you've selected.

5 If you have changed your pointer and you want to change it back to the default pointer, click on the **Default button**.

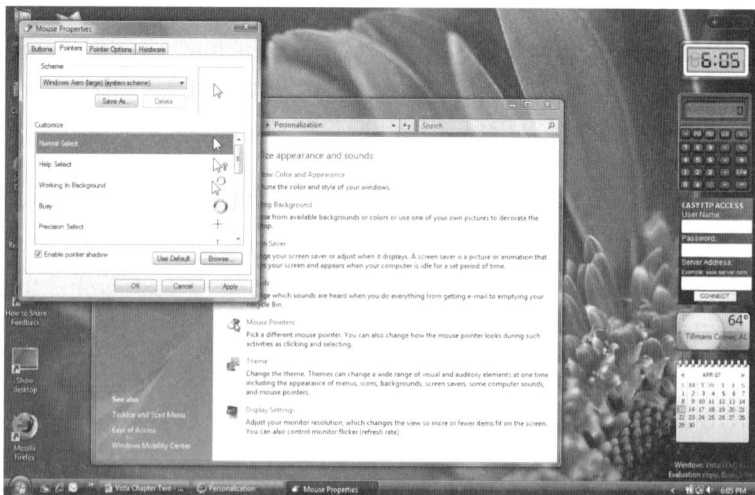

Figure 2.11
Customising your mouse pointer.

6 You can also use customised pointers from a theme that you've installed in Windows Vista. To locate the pointers that apply to that theme, select the **Browse button** and navigate to the location where you stored the theme.

7 Once you've made your pointer selections, click on **Apply** and then click on **OK** to return to the **Personalization dialogue box**.

Selecting a Theme

'Themes' are collections of graphics and sounds that you can use to personalise your computer. Windows Vista comes with a couple of themes installed, but you can also download different themes from the Internet. Using themes to customise your computer is easy. Follow these steps.

1 Right-click on an empty area on your desktop.

2 From the menu that appears, select **Personalize.**

3 Select **Theme** and the **Theme Settings dialogue box** appears, as shown in Figure 2.12.

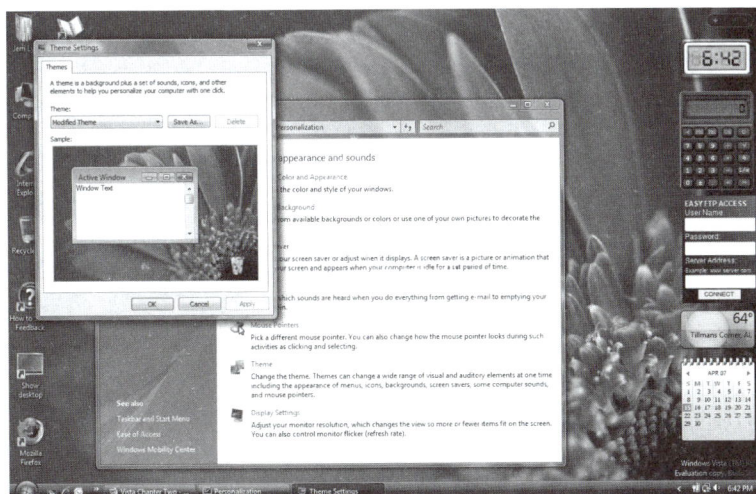

Figure 2.12
Adding a theme will quickly customise your Windows Vista.

4 From the **Theme dropdown menu**, select the theme that you would like to apply. If the theme you want is not listed in the dropdown menu, select **Browse** to navigate to the location of the theme on your hard drive.

5 Once you've selected a theme, click on **Apply** and then select **OK** to return to the **Personalization dialogue box**.

→ Configuring Folder Views

Vista users vary as much from each other as do the people you encounter in everyday life. Everyone works differently, so everyone needs the ability to customise how Vista works for them. One way to do that is to configure folder views to meet your personal preferences. To configure your folder views follow these steps.

1 Go to the **start** menu and select **Control Panel**.

2 In the **Control Panel**, click on **Appearance and Personalization**.

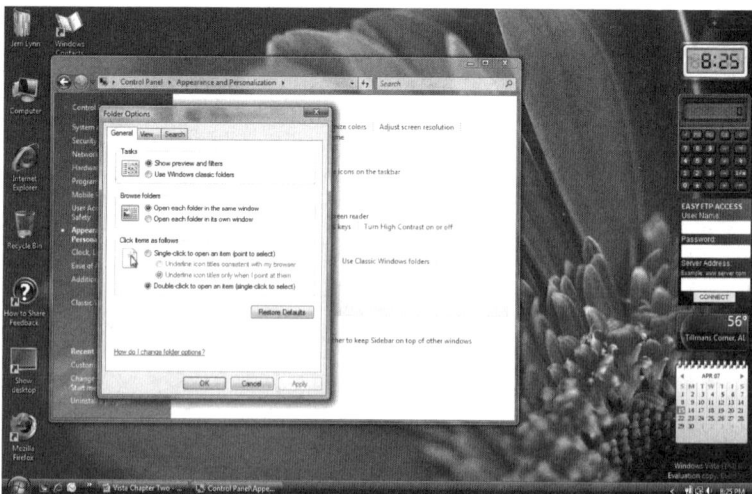

Figure 2.13
Customise your folder options to fit your personal work flow.

3 From the **Personalization dialogue box**, select **Folder Options.** The **Folder Options dialogue box** appears, as shown in Figure 2.13.

4 From the **General tab**, select the desired options for tasks, how you browse folders and what actions are taken when you click on items.

5 The **View tab** has two sections. In the **View section**, you can apply your current folder view (icons, lists and so on) to all folders. In the **Advanced Settings section**, select or deselect options to further customise your folder views.

6 The **Search tab** has options for what to search, how to search and what actions should be taken when non-indexed locations are searched. Select or deselect the desired options.

7 When you've finished making your choices, click on the **Apply button** and then click on **OK** to return to the **Appearance and Personalization dialogue box**.

Timesaver tip

On each of the screens in the **Folder Options dialogue box**, there is a **Restore Defaults button**. If you have made changes to your folder options that you don't like, clicking on the **Restore Defaults button** will return all of your folder options to their default settings.

→ Working with the Windows Sidebar

The Windows sidebar is one of the most useful of the new options in Windows Vista. It is a graphical toolbar that appears on the right side of your screen, as shown in Figure 2.14.

By default, the sidebar is populated with a few simple gadgets,

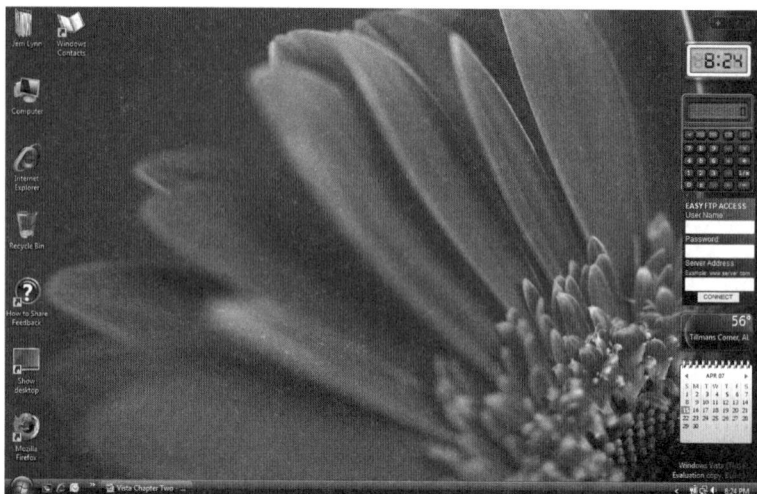

Figure 2.14
The Windows sidebar is one of the new features of Vista.

such as a clock and a picture show. These gadgets can be
changed and rearranged to suit your personal tastes or needs.

Starting the Sidebar

When you boot Vista for the first time, the Windows sidebar
automatically starts. However, if it doesn't appear there, you can
turn it on. To start your Windows sidebar, follow these steps.

1 Go to **Start > Control Panel > Appearance and
Personalization**.

2 Select **Windows Sidebar Properties. The Windows
Sidebar Properties dialogue box** – shown in Figure 2.15 –
appears.

3 Select the box next to the **Start Sidebar when Windows
starts option**.

4 Click on **Apply**, then click on **OK** to return to the
Appearance and Personalization dialogue box.

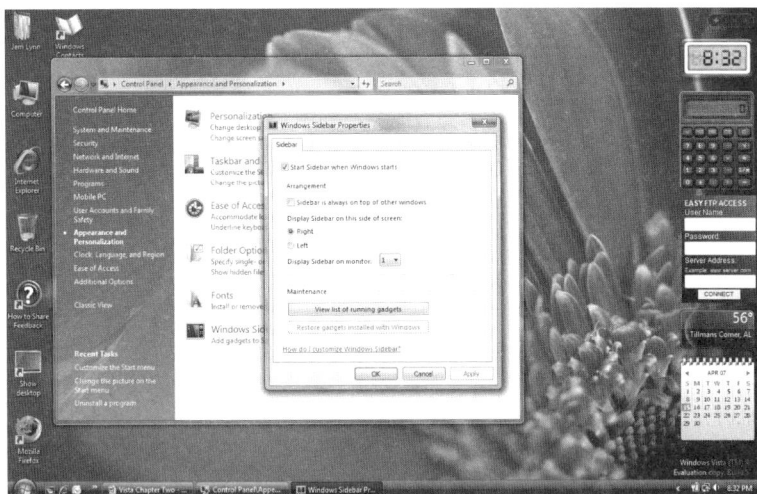

Figure 2.15
Access the Windows Sidebar dialogue box via the control panel.

Configuring the Sidebar

To configure other options on the Windows sidebar, follow these steps.

1 Go to **Start > Control Panel > Appearance and Personalization**.

2 Select **Windows Sidebar Properties**.

3 In the **Windows Sidebar Properties dialogue box**, you can set options for where the sidebar appears – on top of all other windows or not, on the right or on the left. You can also make selections for which monitor your sidebar will appear on if you're using more than one monitor.

4 In the **Maintenance section** of the dialogue box, there is also an option to **View list of running gadgets**. When you click on this button, you're taken to a list of all the gadgets that are active on your sidebar, as shown in Figure 2.16. You can remove any gadget from your sidebar by highlighting it and selecting the **Remove button**.

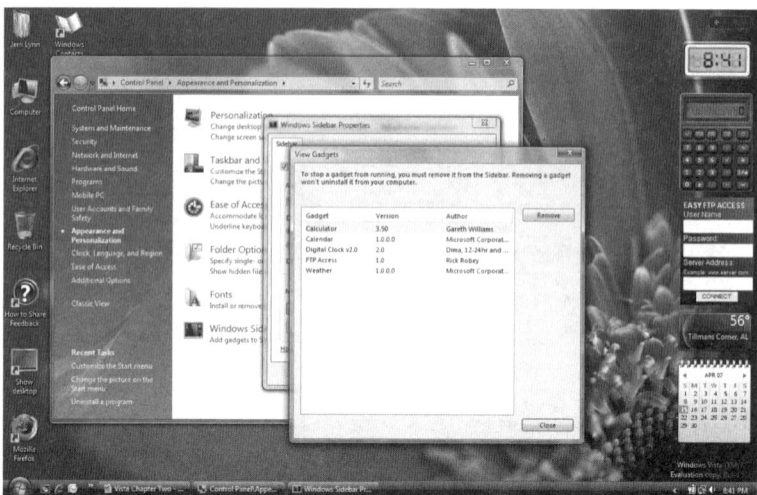

Figure 2.16
Use the list of gadgets to see what's running and remove unwanted gadgets.

5 When you've finished with the list of gadgets, click on the **Close button** to be returned to the **Windows Sidebar Properties dialogue box**.

6 After you have completed your customisation selections, click on the **Apply button**, then click on **OK** to return to the **Appearance and Customisation dialogue box**.

Customising Sidebar Gadgets

The default gadgets on the sidebar may or may not be the right gadgets for you. Windows had dozens of other gadgets for you to choose from and the numbers available for Vista are being increased constantly.

Here's one way to add gadgets to the sidebar.

1 Go to **Start > Control Panel > Appearance and Personalization**.

2 Under **Windows Sidebar Properties**, select **Add gadgets to Sidebar**.

Figure 2.17
Several gadgets have already been installed on your computer.

3 The **Gadget Gallery** – a menu of the gadgets installed on your computer – appears, as shown in Figure 2.17. Double-click on the gadget you'd like to add and it will appear on the sidebar.

4 If the gadget that you're seeking is not available in the Gadget Gallery, click on the **Get more gadgets online link**, located in the lower right corner of the Gadget Gallery. This takes you to the Windows sidebar website, where you can download and install additional gadgets from Microsoft and third-party developers.

5 When you have finished installing your desired gadgets, close **the website** (if open), **Gadget Gallery**, and **Appearance and Personalization dialogue box**. Your chosen gadgets will appear on your sidebar.

Timesaver tip

Another way to access the Gadget Gallery is to click on the **+** (plus icon) at the top of the sidebar. Then, the Gadget Gallery opens and you can add gadgets as detailed above.

If you add a gadget to your sidebar that you later decide you don't want there, removing it is easy. Hover your pointer over the gadget you want to remove. A small toolbar appears on the gadget. Click on the **X** in the toolbar and the gadget is removed from the sidebar.

Some gadgets also have settings that you may need to adjust. For example, a weather gadget will require that you enter your postcode or city or town and county so that the correct weather information is shown for your area. To adjust these settings, hover your pointer over the gadget and, when the toolbar appears on the side of the gadget, click on the spanner icon.

As you can see, customising Vista is easy and, once you've customised the operating system, you'll feel much more comfortable working in Vista. You may also find that your work is much more efficient as a result.

3

Managing Your Computer from the Control Panel

In this lesson you'll learn about working with the Control Panel to add and manage hardware and software, use the administrative tools and access the Backup and Restore Center.

The control panel in Windows Vista is user-friendly and can be learned quickly. Knowing how to navigate in the control panel will help you to manage your computer and files more efficiently.

→ Accessing the Control Panel

To access the control panel, click on the **start menu** and then on **Control Panel**. There are also two other ways to access the Control Panel. In any Vista window, type in the words **Control Panel** in the **address bar** found on the window. That will close the application you are in and open the control panel. You can also access the control panel in most folders from the link on the right side of the page under **Favorite Links**. See Figure 3.1 for the main view of the control panel you will see once it has opened.

The presentation of the control panel in Windows Vista has changed in some ways, but it is still virtually the same. The control panel is divided into categories, with each category presenting a list of tasks that you can perform when that category is open.

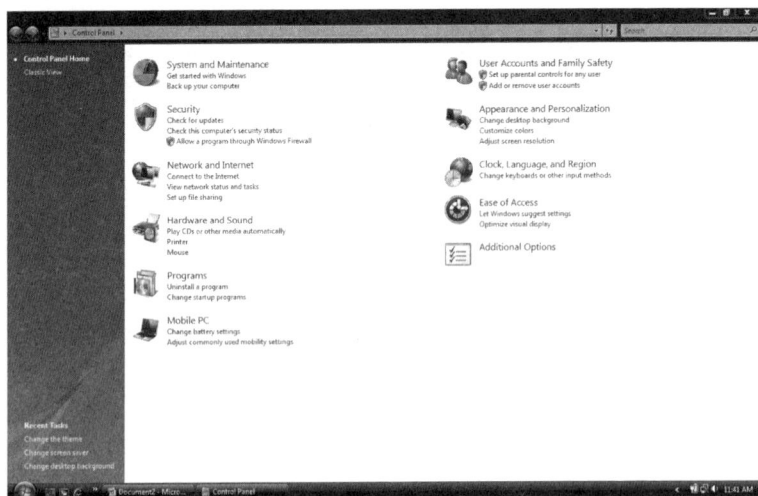

Figure 3.1
The Control panel main view.

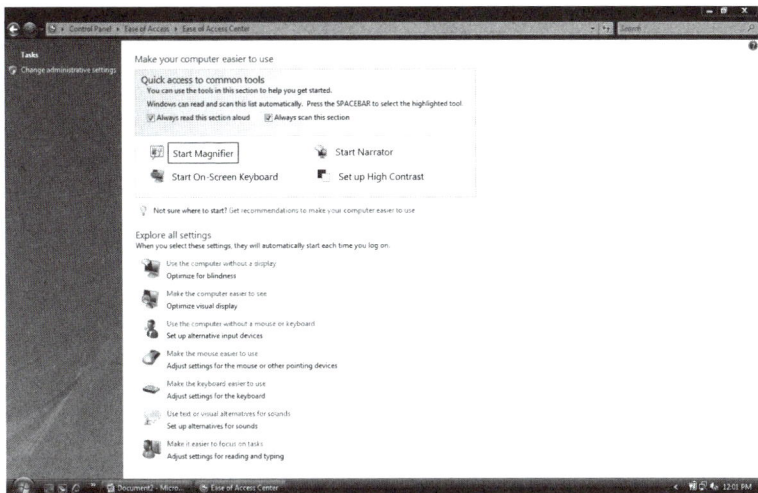

Figure 3.2
The Ease of Access Center allows you to adjust settings for ease of use.

Changing Accessibility Options

In other versions, this option was called "Ease of Accessibility". It is now called "Accessibility Options". These options enable you to configure the computer's overall behaviour to make it easier for people with disabilities to use the computer.

To access the "Ease of Access Center", follow these steps.

1 Go to the **Start menu** and select **Control Panel**.

2 In the control panel, select **Ease of Access**. This will bring you to the **Ease of Access dialogue box**.

3 Select **Ease of Access Center**, as shown in Figure 3.2.

Timesaver tip

When you open the Ease of Access Center, you may hear narration explaining the menu. If you do not wish to hear the narrator, you can mute your sound.

The most commonly used tools for the Ease of Access settings are located at the top of the menu. The following options are available.

- **Magnifier**—This will turn the onscreen magnifier on, which will magnify options on the screen to assist those who are visually impaired.

- **On-Screen Keyboard**—This option will bring up a small onscreen keyboard that can be used with a mouse or other pointing device. This is helpful for people who cannot physically use a keyboard.

- **Narrator**—Once you have turned this option on, opened Windows and dialogue boxes will be read aloud by a narrator and can be heard through the computer's speakers.

- **Set Up High Contrast**—For people who are visually impaired, turning on the high contrast option can be helpful as it can enable them to see opened files and folders.

There are also some less frequently used options given below the tools described above and they can be accessed by clicking on any one of them. These options allow you to quickly change your display to make it easier to read, adjust keyboard and mouse settings and customise how audible alerts behave.

Adding and Managing Hardware

Most of the time, adding hardware in Vista is as simple as connecting the device you want to use to your computer. Windows will install the correct driver information or prompt you to insert the installation disk that came with the hardware. Before you try to install any kind of hardware on your computer, though, you need to be sure that it is compatible with Vista.

Any device that is installed on your computer can be found in the Device Manager, which allows you to manage the hardware that is on your computer. The Device Manager can be found in the Control Panel.

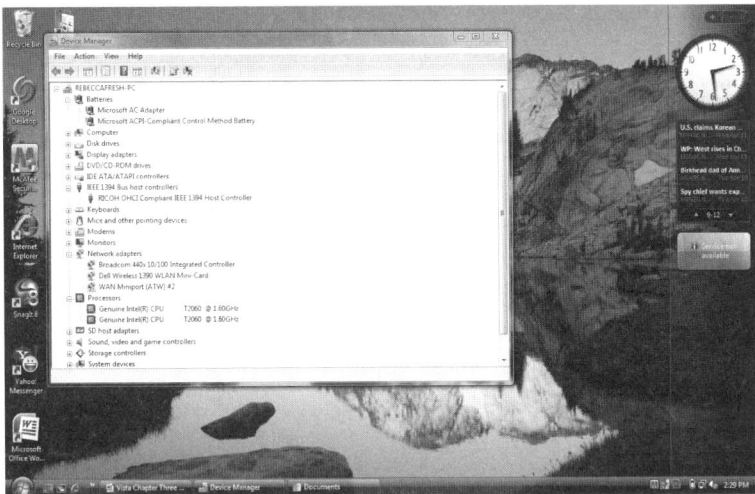

Figure 3.3
The Device Manager menu allows you to manage your hardware.

1 Go to the **Start menu** and then select **Control Panel**.

2 In the Control Panel, click on **Hardware and Sound**. Select the **Device Manager icon**. You will then see the menu for

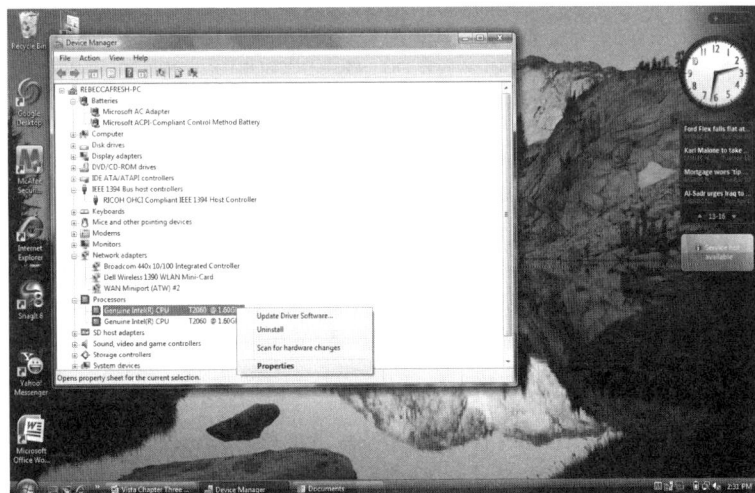

Figure 3.4
Use the Device menu to access device properties.

the **Device Manager**, as shown in Figure 3.3. The menu lists the hardware on your computer in groups.

3 Find the group that your hardware belongs to and click on the + beside that group on the left side.

4 Once the devices come up, right click on the device that you would like to manage. A menu of actions appears.

5 Before managing your hardware, always check the properties of that hardware. To do this, click on **Properties** (see Figure 3.4).

6 Click on the tab that you need to view and use the choices that are presented to you.

7 When you've finished working with your devices, close the Device Manager by clicking on the **X** in the top right corner of the dialogue box. Then close the control panel in the same way.

Adding and Managing Software

Before installing software on your computer, make sure that it is compatible with Windows Vista. Resource requirements are usually listed on the software packaging. To install software, follow these steps.

1 Before installing software on your computer, exit from all running programs.

2 Read the instructions on the back of the packaging for the new software before installing it.

3 Once you have read the enclosed materials, insert the CD into the CD-ROM and follow the onscreen instructions.

To manage your software, follow these steps.

1 Go to the **Control Panel** and click on **Programs**.

2 Select **Programs and Features**. The **Programs dialogue box** appears, as shown in Figure 3.5.

3 Select a program to view the options to **Uninstall**, **Repair** or **Change** that program.

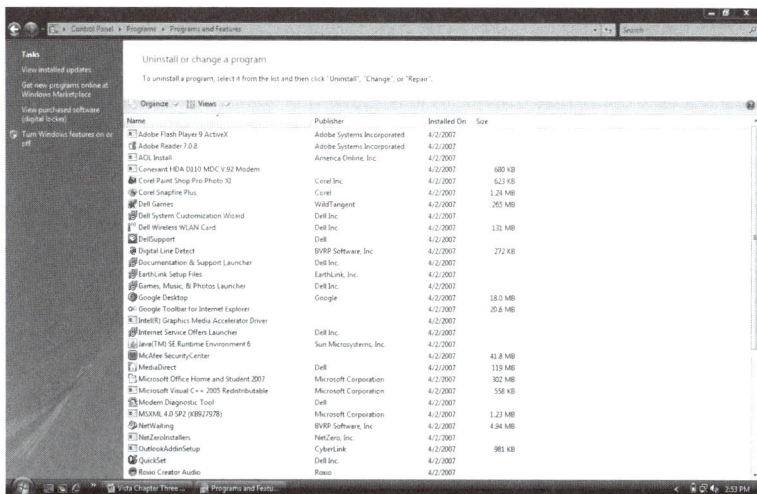

Figure 3.5
The Programs dialogue box is where you add, remove and repair software.

Important

Before uninstalling a program, make sure that it is not necessary to the functioning of your computer. If you're unsure how uninstalling a program will affect your computer's functions, then seek the advice of a professional.

Using the Administrative Tools

The Administrative Tools folder gives you several tool options to help manage your Windows Vista computer.

To access Administrative Tools, take these steps.

1 Go to the **Control Panel**.

2 Select **System and Maintenance**.

3 Select **Administrative Tools** from the list that appears (it is located at the bottom). The **Administrative Tools dialogue box** appears, as shown in Figure 3.6.

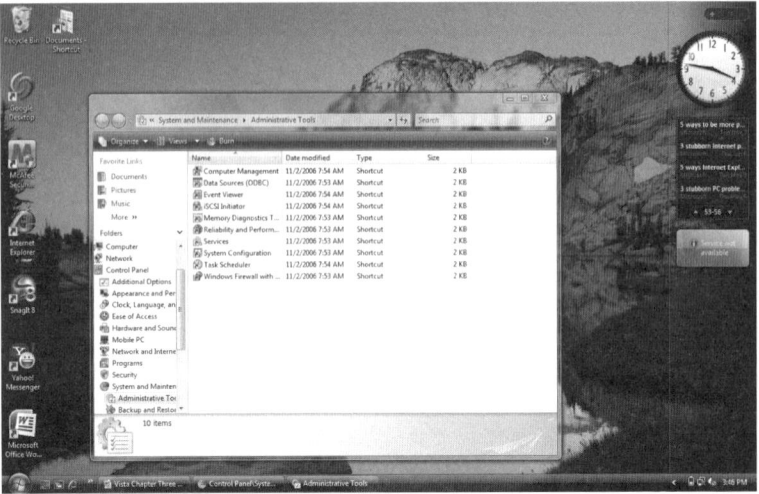

Figure 3.6
The Administrative Tools dialogue box.

The Administrative Tools folder gives you several different
options, such as defragmenting your hard drive and freeing up
disk space. To access these options, click on the menu item that
you would like to view. Each time you click on an item, it will

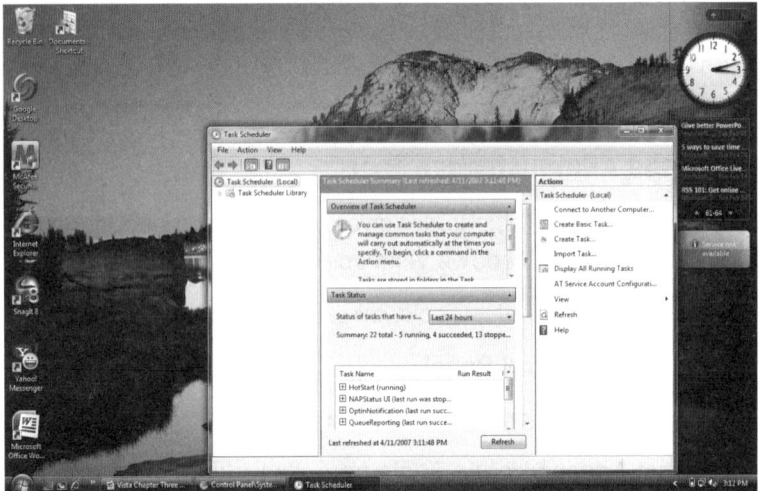

Figure 3.7
The Task Scheduler in Administrative Tools.

bring up a menu such as the one shown in Figure 3.7 for the Task Scheduler.

You can then access the menu tabs to perform the actions you would like to take.

Using AutoPlay

'AutoPlay' tells Vista what to do with different types of media when they are accessed by your computer. To access AutoPlay, do the following.

1 Go to the **Control** Pabnel.

2 Select **Hardware and Sound**. The **Hardware and Sound dialogue box** appears.

3 Select the icon labelled **AutoPlay**. The **AutoPlay dialogue box** appears, as shown in Figure 3.8, which allows you to select the device that is used to play the media you are using.

4 To change the device that is being used, click on the dropdown menu next to each choice and choose the desired device.

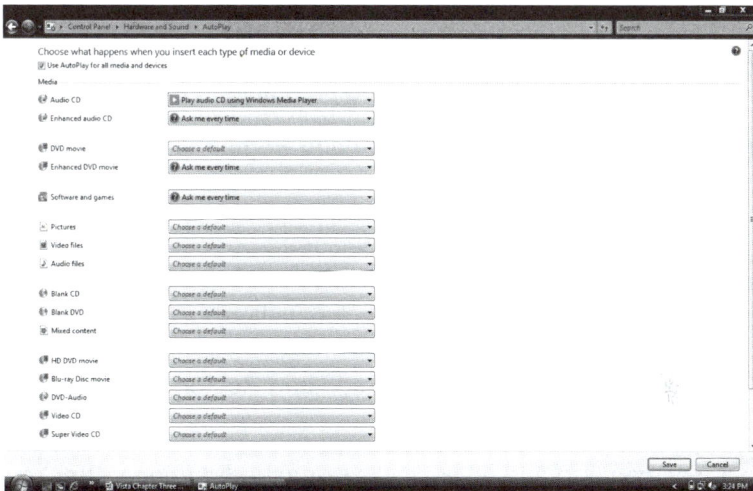

Figure 3.8
The AutoPlay menu.

5 When you have finished changing your settings, click on **Apply** and then **OK** to return to the **Administrative Tools dialogue box**.

Using Date and Time Settings

To change the date and time on your computer and manage how and where they appear, take the following steps.

1 Go to the **Control Panel** and select **Clock, Language and Region**. The **Clock, Language and Region dialogue box** opens.

2 Select **Date and Time**.

3 Select the **Change date and time button** and the **Date and Time Settings dialogue box** appears.

Timesaver tip

You may be prompted to confirm that you want to change your date and time settings. If you are, select **Yes** and you will be taken to the **Date and Time Settings** dialogue box.

---

4 Make the desired changes and then click on **OK** to return to the **Clock, Language and Region dialogue box**.

5 Back on the **Clock, Language and Region dialogue box**, select **Change time zone** and the **Time Zone Settings dialogue box** appears.

6 Use the dropdown menu to select your desired time zone, choose if you want your clock automatically updated for daylight saving time, then click on **OK.** You will then be returned to the **Clock, Language and Region dialogue box**.

7 You can also add other clocks using the **Additional Clocks tab** or choose to have your computer synchronised with Internet time by using the **Internet Time tab**. When you've finished making your selections, click on **Apply** and then click on **OK** to return to the **Clock, Language and Region dialogue box**.

Accessing the Backup and Restore Center

The Backup and Restore Center allows you to take safety precautions, such as backing up your system. Windows Vista can automatically perform this task for you, as well as restoring your system. You can choose to back up certain files and folders on a periodic basis or to back up your entire operating system in case of a computer crash. To create a backup or restore, do the following.

1 Go to **Start > Control Panel**, then select **System and Maintenance**.

2 In the **System and Maintenance dialogue box**, select **Backup and Restore Center**. The **Backup and Restore Center dialogue box** appears, as shown in Figure 3.9.

3 In the **Backup and Restore Center menu**, select **Back up files** to back up certain files on your computer or **Back up**

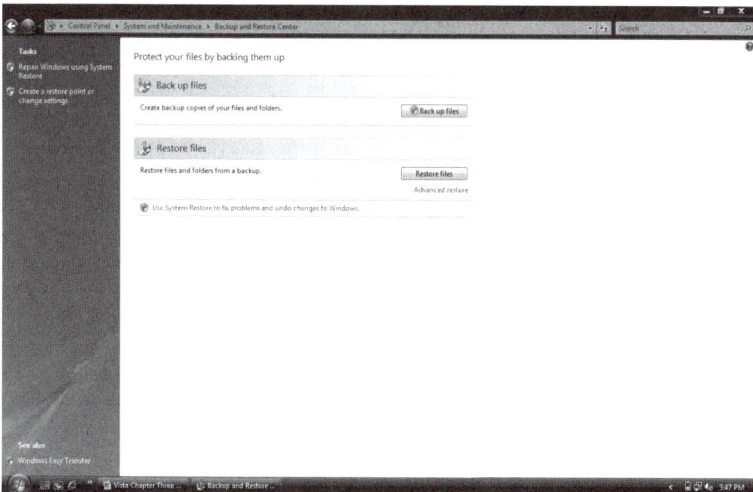

Figure 3.9
The Backup and Restore Center dialogue box.

computer to back up all of the programs, applications and files on your computer.

Timesaver tip

You may be prompted to grant permission to continue with the backup process. Click on **Yes** and you will proceed to the **Backup Wizard**.

---

4 Use the Wizard that appears for both options to complete your backup.

5 To perform a restore, select **Restore files** to restore the files that you have in back up or **Restore computer** to restore your whole system.

6 A **Restore Wizard** walks you through the restoration process.

Important

You may be prompted to confirm that you want to complete the restoration process. Use caution when confirming this action and make sure that all files and programs have been properly backed up before continuing. In some cases, the restoration will result in you losing all files that are stored on your computer.

Using BitLocker Drive Encryption

The BitLocker Drive Encryption program allows you to encrypt chosen folders and files that you want protected to keep others from viewing them, even if they are using a password-cracking program. This is a great security feature when you have sensitive data on your computer.

To use the BitLocker Drive Encryption program, you need to make sure that your computer meets the minimum requirements for it. The computer will need at least two partitions and both partitions will need to be formatted with NT File System (NTFS) protocols.

To turn on the BitLocker Drive Encryption program, do the following.

1 Select **Start > Control Panel**.

2 In the **Control Panel menu** select **Security**. The **Security dialogue box** appears.

3 Select **BitLocker Drive Encryption**. The **BitLocker Drive Encryption dialogue box** appears.

4 Select **Turn on BitLocker** and then use the **Bitlocker Wizard** that appears to complete the activation process.

Setting Folder Options

Folder options enable you to set up how folders look and what actions are taken when the folders are open. You can access folder options in one of two ways. These are either via the control panel or from any folder in Windows Vista. To access folder options from a folder, select **Organize** on the top left of the folder screen. Then, choose **Folder Options**. This opens the **Folder Options dialogue box**, shown in Figure 3.10.

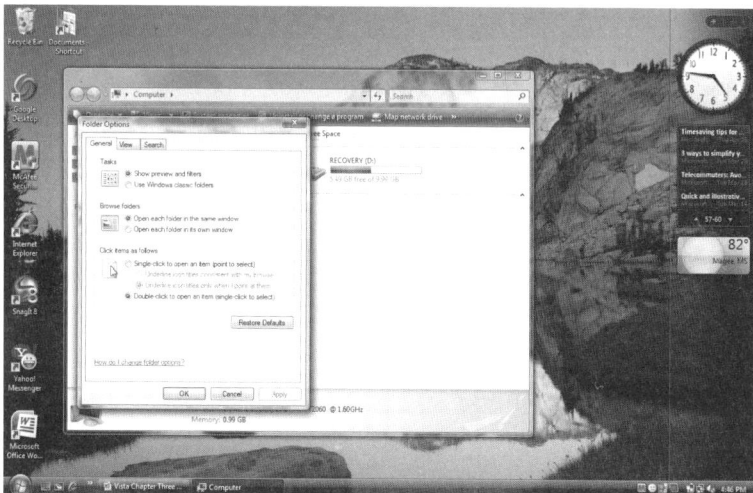

Figure 3.10
The Folder Options dialogue box.

There are three tabs in the **Folder Options dialogue box** – namely, General, View and Search. Each tab allows you to customise your folders in different ways.

- **General**—Use this tab to make the major appearance changes. With Tasks, you can choose if you want to show previews and filters of the folder or the classic Windows folders. For the optimum use of Vista, the previews and filters option is the best choice. Browse Folders allows you to choose if your folders each open on a separate window or in the same window. Opening them in the same window will help to keep your taskbar from filling up. The Click items that follow are self-explanatory.

- **View**—The View tab allows you to choose how you would like to view your folders. Choose the tick boxes that you would like applied to your folder. To save your changes, click on **Apply** and **OK**. Notice that you have a choice as to whether to apply the view to all your folders or just the one you have opened.

- **Search**—The Search tab is used to customise the way that you would like your computer to use Search in a folder. The options given are self-explanatory.

Figure 3.11
The Default Programs menu.

Managing Default Programs

You can manage default programs by going to the **Start menu** and selecting **Default Programs**, which is located to the right under **Control Panel**. The Default Programs menu lets you choose the programs that Windows uses as defaults (see Figure 3.11). Keep in mind that changing any of these settings will change the defaults that Vista will use to handle certain programs and file types.

Setting Indexing Options

Windows Vista uses indexing to search for documents, folders, photos and other files more quickly than is possible otherwise. The indexing options in Vista can be modified to do such things as indexing encrypted files or certain file types.

To access the indexing options, take the following steps.

1 Go to the **Control Panel** and type **Indexing Options** in the search field. The **Indexing Options icon** will then appear.

2 Select **Indexing Options** to view the dialogue box shown in Figure 3.12.

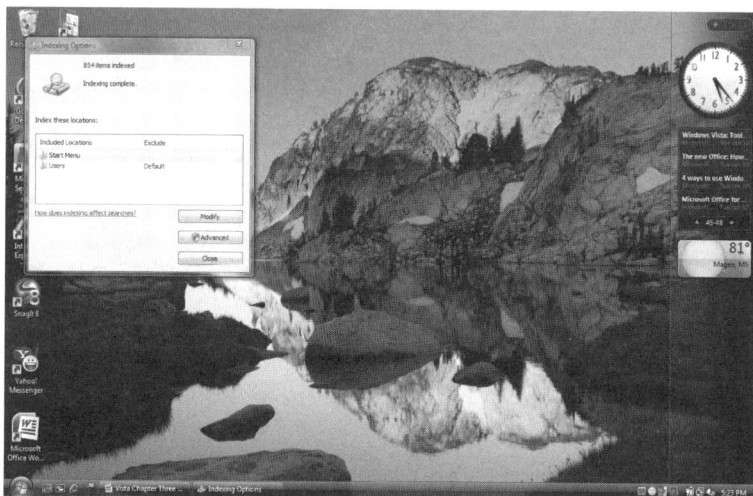

Figure 3.12
The Indexing Options window.

3 Highlight the area that you would like to change and click on **Modify.** The **Indexed Locations dialogue box** for that area appears.

4 Make the desired changes and then click on **OK.** You will be returned to the **Indexing Options dialogue box**.

5 You can also select **Advanced** to change advanced options such as file settings and file types.

6 When you have finished, click on **OK** to save your changes and return to the **Indexing Options dialogue box**.

7 Click on **Close** and close the **Control Panel** when you have finished.

Managing Font Selections

There is a fonts folder located in the control panel that allows you to manage the fonts your computer uses. To access the fonts folder, take these steps.

1 Go to the **Control Panel**.

2 Select **Appearance and Personalization**.

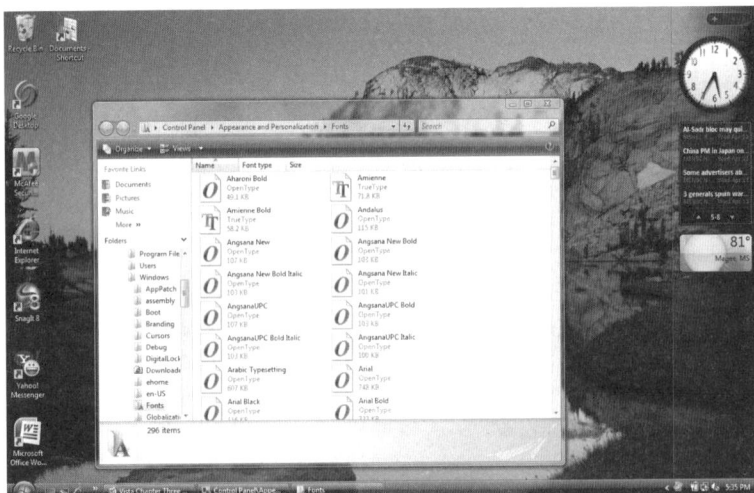

Figure 3.13
The Fonts window.

3 Select **Fonts**. This brings up the **Fonts dialogue box**, which shows all the fonts that are available (see Figure 3.13).

4 Use this dialogue box to view the different fonts available on your computer. You can also print and delete fonts from this folder.

3

Important

Changing the fonts in Vista can change the way your applications appear. Some fonts display better onscreen than others, and some fonts display better in print. If you choose to change the fonts, you can use the Display property dialogue box. To preview, double-click the font.

4

Connecting to the Internet

In this lesson you'll learn about broadband and dial-up Internet connections, how to install and configure a modem and connect to the Internet.

→ Understanding Internet Connections

If you are a novice Internet user, you may not know the ins and outs of connecting to the Internet. Understanding Internet connections makes the installation and use of the Internet an easier and more enjoyable task.

Broadband Internet Connections

Because of the slow speed of dial-up connections due to the larger sizes of web pages, for this method of connection to the Internet, many people use broadband. The three main types of broadband Internet connections are cable, DSL and satellite. Here is a quick overview of each type.

- **Cable**—For those with cable, the cable line that feeds your TV can also (if it is available in your area) be used to access the Internet. The company will either rent you a cable modem, which connects to your cable and then to your computer via a USB or ethernet port, or you can purchase one from most electronics or computer shops. Cable Internet access can provide you with a much faster service than can dial-up. The speed will depend on the cable company and the number of users accessing the Internet via the same cable as you.

- **DSL**—DSL which stands for digital subscriber line, is provided by a telephone company. DSL is the most popular type of broadband Internet connection because of its enhanced speed. DSL, like cable Internet access, may not be available in all areas. To use DSL, you must have an adapter that hooks into your phone line and is then run to your computer via the ethernet or USB port on your computer. The DSL provider will offer to sell or rent you the adapter or you can purchase one separately. With DSL, you can also purchase a wireless modem that you can run to your DSL modem to allow you wireless access from other computers in the household (if they are equipped with wireless cards).

- **Satellite**—Satellite Internet access uses a small dish mounted to your home (just like the ones used for satellite TV). Information is sent from an aerial satellite to your satellite dish, which allows you to have Internet access. You must have a clear view of the sky to use this service. The satellite provider should send you the accessories that you need to use this kind of connection.

4

The costs of broadband Internet services vary, depending on the type of services you choose and the prices charged by different service providers.

Dial-up Internet Connections

For those who don't have access to broadband, dial-up Internet connection services are usually readily available. These services are provided by your phone company or other companies such as AOL. Dial-up Internet connections are less expensive than broadband.

With dial-up, you are required to have at least a 56K modem. If you have recently purchased a computer, you probably have an internal modem already installed on it and all that needs to be done is for a phone line to be connected to your computer.

If you have to purchase a modem, however, be sure to check that it is at least 56K and that you have what you need to connect it to your phone line and computer. Normally you will need a phone line splitter and an extra phone line cable. You will probably also need to get an ethernet cable if the modem does not come with one.

Any operating system from Windows XP up to Windows Vista has a setup Wizard to help you set up the driver for the modem and access to the Internet. If you are purchasing a modem, be sure to read the instructions carefully before you install it and ensure that your computer is equipped for that particular modem.

→ Installing and Configuring a Modem

Because modems are standard hardware now, most computers have internal modems already installed when you buy them. If, however, you have to use an external modem, installing it should be as easy as plugging it in. When you purchase a modem, be sure that it is compatible with your computer and operating system and choose a "plug and play" device. Then you should be able to just plug it in to your USB and ethernet drive and the computer will then automatically recognise and install it.

Once installed, you need to configure the modem, as follows.

1 Go to the **Control Panel**.

2 Select **Hardware and Sound**.

3 Then, select the **Phone and Modem Options icon**. This opens the **Phone and Modem Options dialogue box**. Use the options shown to set up your dialing rules, starting with the location information, shown in Figure 4.1.

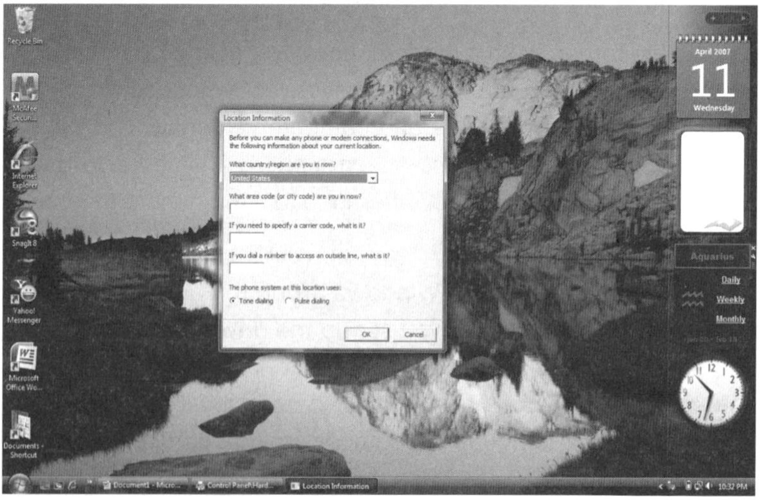

Figure 4.1
The Location Information window.

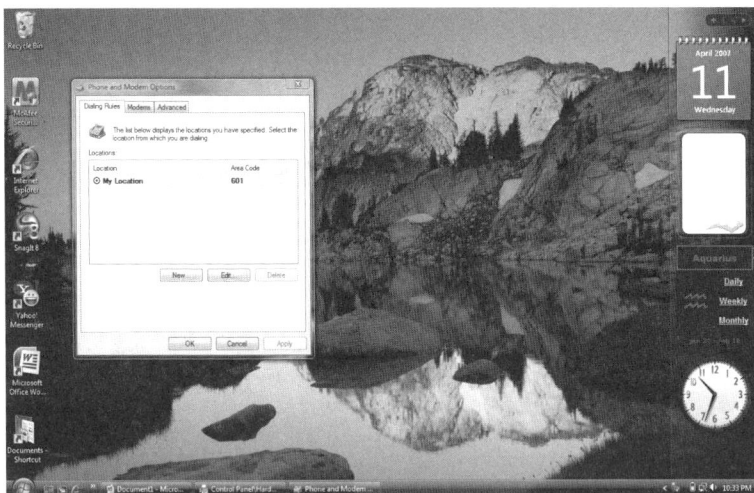

Figure 4.2
The Phone and Modem Options window.

4 Once you have filled out the information in this window, click
on **OK** to be taken to the next window, which is the **Phone
and Modem Options**, shown in Figure 4.2.

There are three tabs at the top of this window – Dialing Rules,
Modems and Advanced. The following is a brief explanation of
each of them.

- **Dialing Rules**—Here you can add a new location or edit a
current location. When you edit a new location, you will see
the screen shown in Figure 4.3. The information that needs to
be filled in here is self-explanatory. There are also Area Code
Rules and Calling Card tabs in this menu and these are self-
explanatory. When you have entered the information in each
screen, be sure to click on **Apply** and **OK** to save your
settings.

- **Modems**—When you click on the Modems tab, you will see
three options that you can choose from. You can adjust the
modem's speaker volume by using the slider tab (a lower
volume here is usually sufficient), use the dropdown menu for

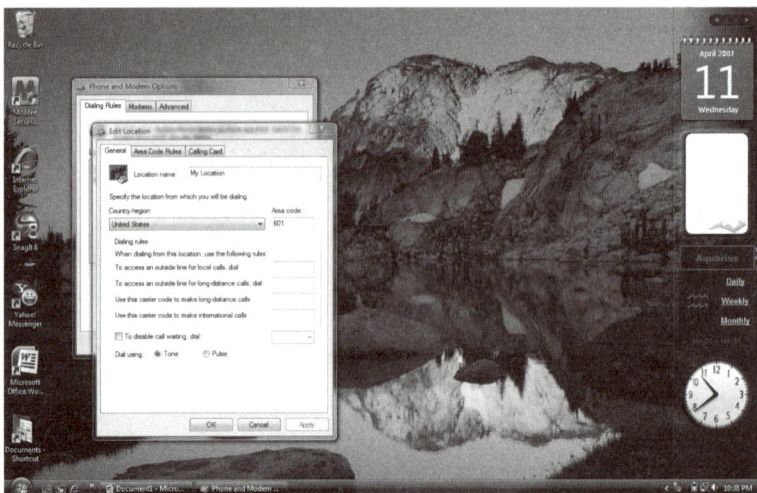

Figure 4.3
The Edit Location screen.

the Maximum Port Speed to set the maximum connection speed that you wish the modem to connect at (it is best to leave this on the default setting) and the Dial Control section has a tick box for Wait for Dial Tone Before Dialing. The last option will probably already be enabled and should stay enabled so that your modem checks for a dial tone before trying to connect.

■ **Advanced**—This tab will give you an Extra Settings field where you can enter additional modem string commands. Unless the documentation that comes with your modem specifically tells you to change the settings here, they should be left as they are.

→ Connecting to the Internet

Once you have set up your DSL modem (and wireless modem if you will be using a wireless Internet connection) or set up your dial-up settings, you are ready to connect to the Internet.

To do this, simply double-click on the Internet Explorer icon on your desktop (or the program icon for your Internet service provider) and follow the instructions provided for dial-up. If you're connecting via DSL or cable, you should be able to start surfing immediately.

4

5

Using Internet Explorer

In this lesson you'll learn how to explore and navigate in Internet Explorer, organise Favourites and use Internet Explorer Tabs.

→ Exploring Internet Explorer

Internet Explorer (IE) is Vista's built in web browser that allows you to connect to and explore the Internet. It is represented by a blue letter "e" icon on your desktop.

Opening the Browser

To open the Internet Explorer browser and connect to the Internet, double-click on the **Internet Explorer icon** located on your desktop. If you are using a broadband Internet service, this action should automatically connect you to the Internet. If you are a dial-up user, you will have to click on **Connect** when the browser box pops up on the screen.

> ### Timesaver tip
>
> Most Internet service providers (ISPs) have a software application that you install when you begin using their services. If you have such an application from your ISP, you can also use that icon instead to connect to the Internet.

Navigating in Internet Explorer

When you open Internet Explorer, your home page should appear in the browser window, as shown in Figure 5.1.

At the top left of the window, just below the Internet Explorer icon, you will find the back and forward buttons and the address bar. These allow you to view previous web pages, go forward to the next page or type an address in the bar to take you to another page. There are several icons across the top of the window that allow you to personalise your Internet experience in many ways. Notice at the bottom right corner that there is a message letting you know you are on the Internet and, whether or not you are in protected mode. There is also a zoom option available, to the right of the protection message.

Figure 5.1
You can change your Internet Explorer home page.

Using Home Settings

The web page that your computer opens up to when you connect to the Internet is your home page. A default page exists in Internet Explorer, but you have the option to change the home page to a website that suits your needs better.

There is a small house in the bar on the right that takes you to your home page when you click on it. There is also a dropdown menu attached to the icon that gives you options for your home page, as shown in Figure 5.2.

To change your home page, do the following.

1 Navigate to the website that you would like to use as your home page.

2 Open the home page dropdown menu.

3 Select **Add or Change Home Page**. The **Add or Change Home Page dialogue box** appears.

4 Choose whether or not to make the current page your home page or add it to your home page tabs.

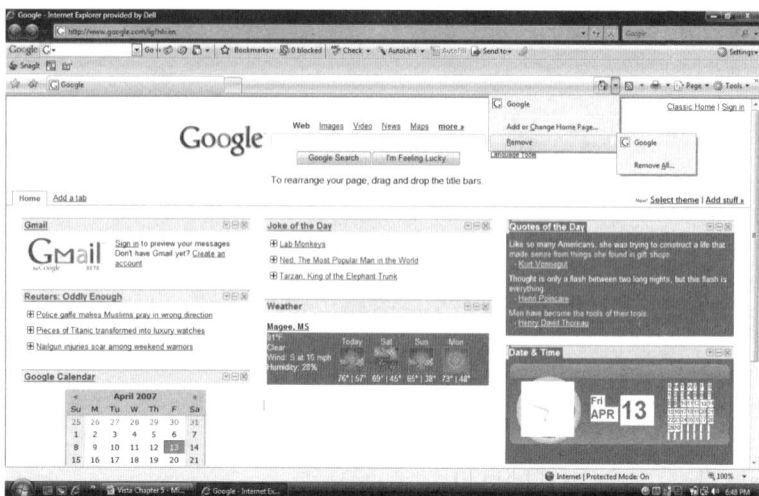

Figure 5.2
Home Page options.

Timesaver tip

With the new Internet Explorer, you can have multiple home pages. Each home page opens in a different tab, so when you click on the home page icon, all of the home pages you have selected are opened in different tabs.

If you have selected a home page that you now want to change or delete, just take the following steps.

1 Open **Internet Explorer**.

2 Open the **home page dropdown menu**.

3 Select **Remove** and then click on the page you want to remove. You can also click on **Remove All** to remove all of the home pages that you have set.

Organising Favourites

The star icon to the left of the window is called the Favorites

Figure 5.3
Favorites Center with Feeds and History buttons.

Center. Click on this icon to see the websites that you have added to your favourites list. You can also access your history and RSS feeds (see under "Understanding Feeds and Printing" below), as shown in Figure 5.3.

To save a website to your favourites list, do the following.

1 Navigate to the web page that you want to add to your favourites list.

2 Click on the icon to the left of the address bar that has a plus sign (+) located over it.

3 This opens a menu from which you should select **Add to Favorites**. The **Add a Favorite dialogue box** appears.

4 Type a name for the link in the text box provided. By default, the name of the website should appear in this box.

5 Using the **Create in: dropdown menu**, select the folder that you would like the favourite added to.

6 If you would like to create a new folder for your favourite, click on the **New Folder button** and then add a name to your folder and tell Internet Explorer where to put it. Click on **Create** to create the folder.

7 When you're returned to the **Add a Favorite dialogue box**, click on **Add** and the web page will be added to your favourites list in the location you have specified.

Using Internet Explorer Tabs

Something new in Internet Explorer is the tabbed browsing capability. Figure 5.4 shows where the tabs are located on your browser. To start, you have one tab, labelled "Home". Next to it the words "Add a tab" indicate that you can add other tabs. All you have to do is click on those words and a new, full-size tab is opened.

Timesaver tip

A faster way to open a blank tab is to use the keyboard combination **Ctrl + T**.

Figure 5.4
Internet Explorer now has tabbed browsing.

Once a tab is open, you can navigate to any website from it by typing the web address into the address bar and pressing **ENTER** on your keyboard or clicking on the double arrow button on the right side of the address bar.

Timesaver tip

A faster way to open a new tab is to type a website address in the address bar and then press the keyboard combination **Alt + ENTER**. This will open the website in a new tab.

Understanding Feeds and Printing

If you subscribe to any kind of really simple syndication (RSS) feeds, the Feeds button allows you to access those feeds. Like the Home button, the Feeds button has a dropdown menu that allows you to choose which feed you would like to access.

Unfortunately, adding a feed to Internet Explorer is not as simple as it should be. Before you can add a feed to the RSS reader, you must first install a plug-in that enables the options you need in order to add the feed.

To install the plug-in, follow these steps.

1 Open **Internet Explorer**.

2 Select the **Tools dropdown menu** on the right side of Internet Explorer.

3 Choose **Manage Add-ons** and select **Find More Add-ons**.

4 You are taken to a Microsoft website where you can search for a feed reader. When you find the one that you want to use, click on **Download Now.**

5 The **Download dialogue box** appears. Select **Run** and the program will be downloaded and then the **Installation Wizard** will begin.

6 Once the installation has been completed, go back to your browser window and select **Tools > Manage Add-ons > Enable or Disable Add-ons.**

7 The **Manage Add-ons dialogue box** appears. Select the feed reader that you have just installed and click on **Enable** in the **Settings box**.

8 Click on **OK** and the feed reader should appear on your Internet Explorer toolbar.

9 Then, to add feeds to your reader, follow the directions provided for the toolbar you have selected.

Accessing and Using Internet Explorer Tools

In the right side of the Internet Explorer toolbar is a tab labelled "Tools". You can access Internet Explorer's tools by clicking on the down arrow to bring up the dropdown Tools menu, as shown in Figure 5.5.

Below is a brief overview of what you can do with Internet Explorer's tools.

Figure 5.5
The Tools Menu.

- **Delete Browsing History**—This option allows you to delete all web pages that have been stored in History.

- **Diagnose Connection Problems**—If you having problems with your Internet connection or surfing on the Internet, this option lets Windows diagnose the possible problems with your connection.

- **Pop-up Blocker**—This option allows you turn the pop-up blocker on or off and the Settings option lets you choose which sites to allow pop-ups from, if any.

- **Phishing Filter**—Though this option will let you turn the phishing filter off, it is recommended that you leave it on. This filter works to identify false web pages that could potentially cause you harm by stealing your personal information.

- **Manage Add-ons**—If you use add-ons, you can manage them using this option.

- **Work Offline**—If you wish to work without an Internet connection, this option will allow you to do so.

- **Windows Update**—This option allows you to set up the schedule that you would like to follow to look for and download any Windows updates that are available.

- **Full Screen**—This option lets you view Internet Explorer in full screen mode. You will no longer see your toolbar, but you can place your mouse pointer over the top of the screen and your toolbar will reappear. You can also access the full screen option by pressing F11 at the top of your keyboard.

- **Menu Bar**—This allows you to turn your menu bar at the top of the Window on or off.

- **Toolbars**—Create a custom toolbar by accessing this option. It will also adjust Internet Explorer's default toolbars.

- **Send to OneNote and SunJava Console**—This allows you to send a page to OneNote or your SunJava Console.

5

■ **Internet Options**—This gives you many other options for managing Internet Explorer.

→ Configuring Internet Options

Internet Options is found in the Tools menu. To open Internet Options, go to **Tools** and select **Internet Options**, at the bottom of the menu. There are seven tabs to choose from in this menu.

Using the General Tab

The General tab (shown in Figure 5.6) contains the categories Home page, Browsing history, Search, Tabs and Appearance.

Here is a brief description of how these categories can be used.

■ **Home page**—You can change your home page here by typing in a new URL in the address field. Your home page is the page that Internet Explorer automatically opens up to when you connect to the Internet.

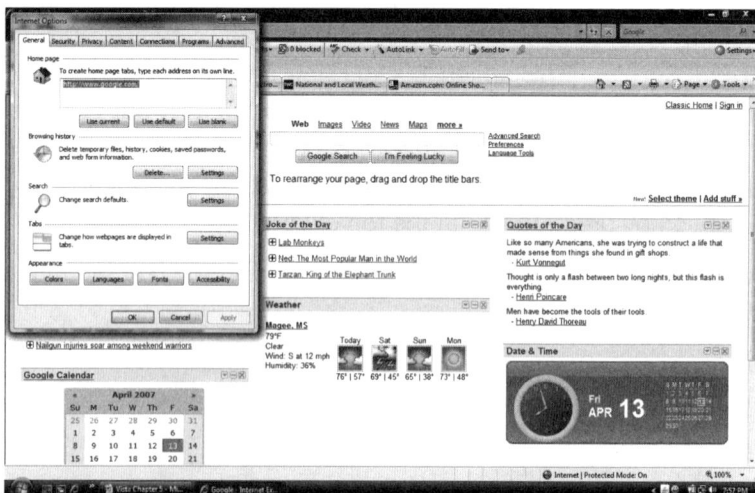

Figure 5.6
The General tab.

- **Browsing history**—You can delete your browsing history from here and decide how Internet pages are stored. How you configure these settings will determine how you will view a previously visited site.

- **Search**—This allows you to add or remove search engines. The Vista search engine is MSN by default, but if you want to change it to, say, Google Search, you can do so by adding it to your choice of search engines.

- **Tabs**—This section will allow you to change how web pages are displayed on your Internet Explorer tabs. You can select or deselect your choices by clicking on the tick boxes next to those choices. The default settings are usually all you will need if you are not comfortable with changing these settings.

- **Appearance**—You can go in here and change the overall look of your Internet Explorer and the way web pages are displayed. The options available should be self-explanatory.

Using the Security Tab

The Security tab allows you to set and change your security settings for Internet Explorer. As you can see in Figure 5.7, you

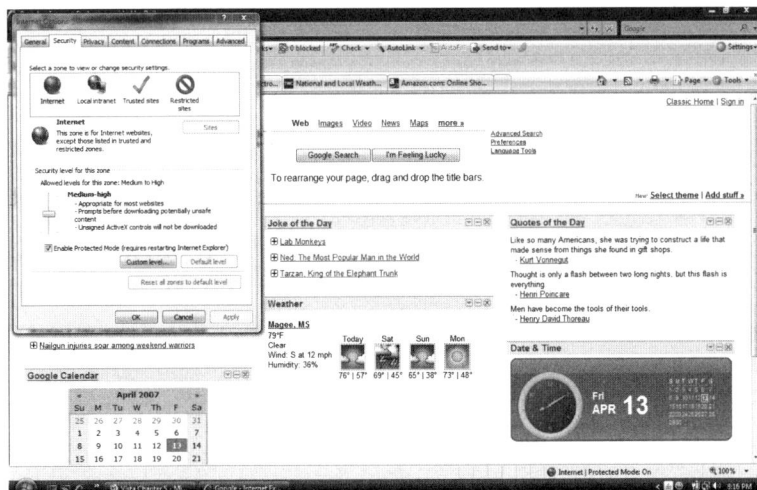

Figure 5.7
The Security tab.

can view any zone to change the settings, as well as set the security level that you are most comfortable with. The default security level setting is medium. If you are set up on a network, you should not change any security settings unless instructed to do so by your network administrator.

Using the Privacy Tab

This tab gives you a slider bar option to choose the amount of privacy you would like to have when you are surfing on the Internet (see Figure 5.8). When you visit a website, it tries to collect information about you and your computer. The security setting that you choose determines what kind of information can be gathered. The default setting for privacy is medium, which is usually all that you will need.

There is also a settings button for a pop-up blocker. It will let you change which (if any) pop-ups you will allow to pop up.

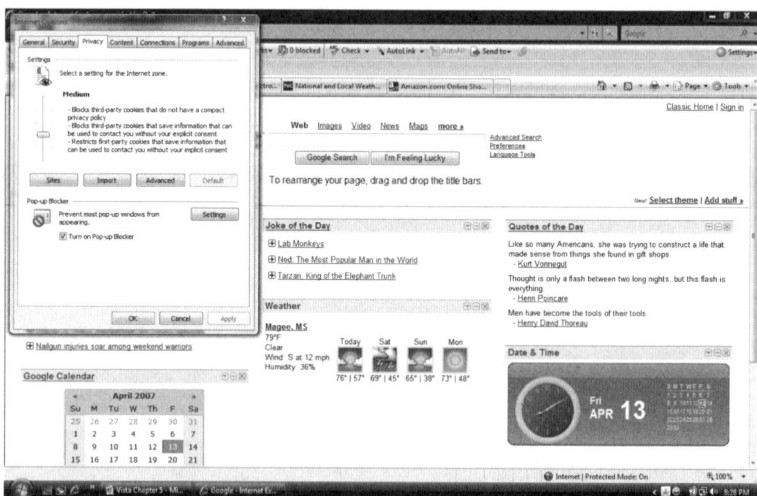

Figure 5.8
The Privacy tab.

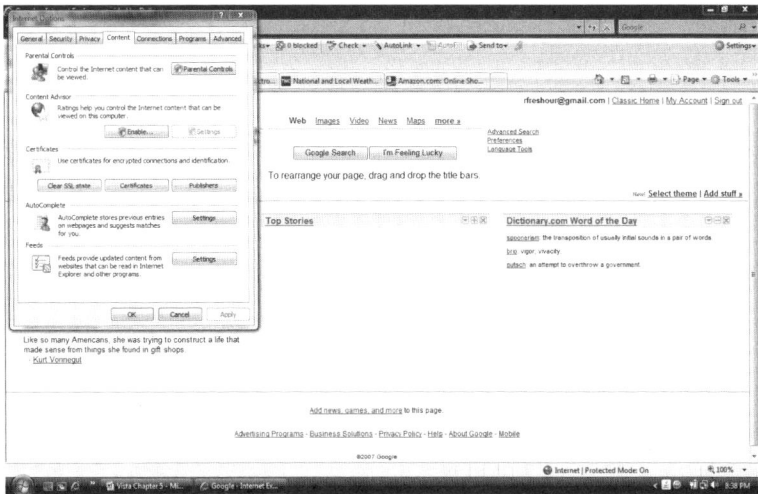

Figure 5.9
The Content tab.

Using the Content Tab

The Content tab (shown in Figure 5.9) lets you configure how different kinds of content are managed by Internet Explorer.

The Parental Controls option allows you to control the content that your children look at while they are on the Internet. The Content Advisor option gives you ratings that help you control the content that is being viewed. If you are a home user, the Certificates options are not something that you need to bother with. Equally, if you are on a network, they do not need to be changed unless you are instructed to do so by your network administrator.

AutoComplete gives you the option to store previous entries that you have made in order to give you suggestions when typing information in the future. For example, if you have user log-ins on several different sites and your user name is the same for all of them, say "Jane Smith", as soon as you start typing the user name, it will automatically give you suggestions that you can choose instead of having to type the entire name.

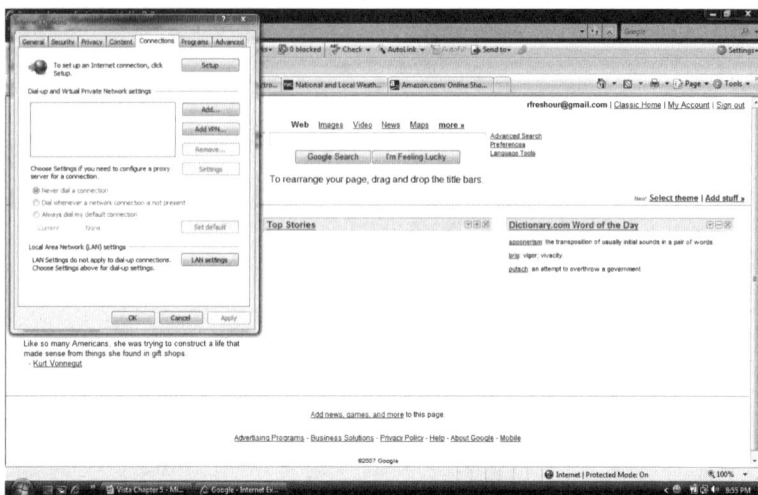

Figure 5.10
The Connections tab.

The Settings button in the Feeds option allows you to set up a schedule for how frequently feeds will be downloaded if you choose to receive them. These settings are self-explanatory.

Using the Connections Tab

The Connections tab enables you to set up your Internet connection. If you are a dial-up customer, you can add or delete dial-up network settings and configure how and when to dial a connection.

There is also a button for LAN settings, which is what wireless Internet users need to configure if they do not want to use the manual settings (see Figure 5.10).

Using the Programs Tab

In Figure 5.11 you can see the Programs tab. This tab lets you choose which programs in Vista perform what options.

The default web browser settings do not need to be changed. If you use add-ons, they can be managed by clicking on the

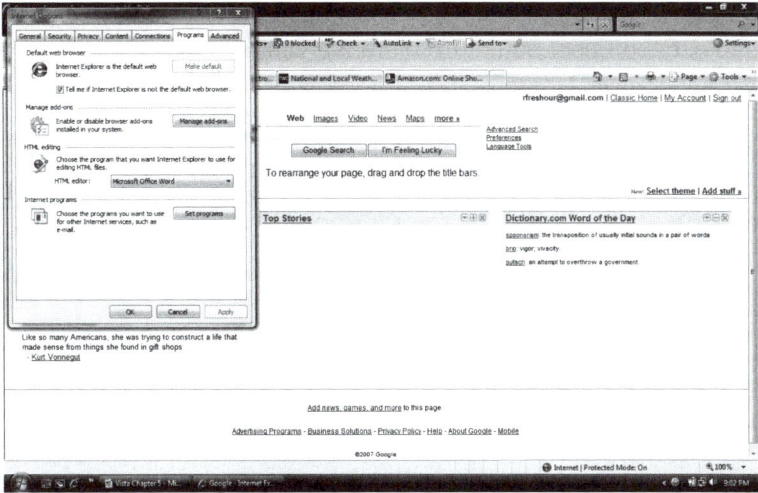

Figure 5.11
The Programs tab.

Manage add-ons button. The HTML editing button enables you
to choose the program that you want Internet Explorer to use for
editing HTML files. The Internet programs setting allows you to
choose which programs you wish to use for Internet services
such as e-mail. For example, if you choose to send an e-mail
while you are visiting a web page, Internet Explorer will
automatically open Windows Mail. However, you may have
another e-mail account that you would rather use. This setting
allows you to choose that other account as the account will
open when you are visiting a web page and want to send an
e-mail.

Using the Advanced Tab

The Advanced tab (see Figure 5.12) gives you a list of choices
with tick boxes by them so that you can choose a variety of
processes. Use caution when changing these settings as they
can affect the performance of your computer. The default
settings are usually sufficient for all activities. However, if you do

change any of them and you are not happy with the results, you can use the Reset button to return the settings back to the default choices.

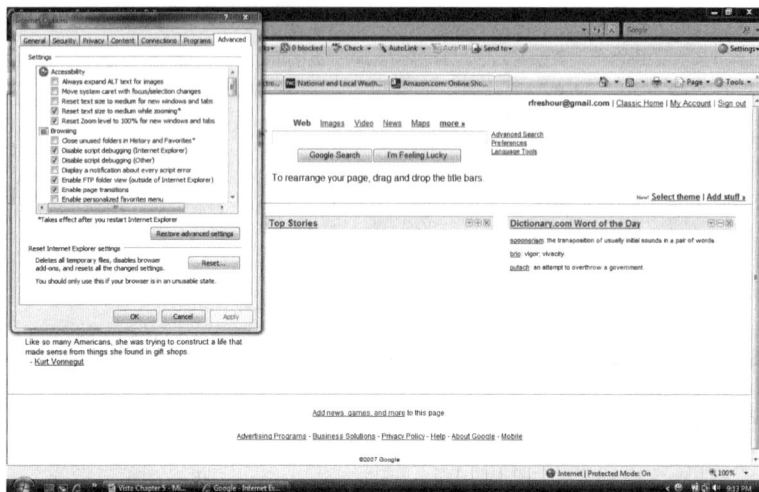

Figure 5.12
The Advanced tab.

6

Using Windows Mail

In this lesson you'll how to create and manage Mail Accounts in Windows Mail including how to send and receive mail and attachments, use the Address Book and work with Contacts.

→ Setting Up Windows Mail

Windows Mail is the new version of Microsoft Outlook – the mail-handling program for the Vista operating system. In previous editions of Microsoft operating systems, this feature was called Outlook Express.

To open your Windows Mail program, go to **Start > All Programs** and select **Windows Mail**. The first time your mailbox opens, a message from Microsoft is displayed, even if you have not been connected to the Internet. This message is a quick explanation of how to get started using Windows Mail.

Creating Mail Accounts

The first time that you open Windows Mail, you will be prompted to create a mail account. If you do not set up your mail account then, you can set it up at any time by using these steps.

1 Open **Windows Mail**.

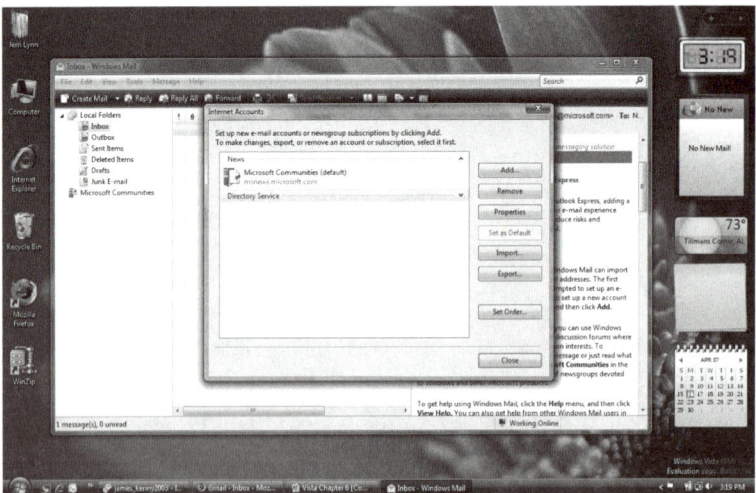

Figure 6.1
Use the Internet Accounts dialogue box to create a new e-mail account.

2 Go to **Tools** and select **Accounts** from the menu that appears.

3 As shown in Figure 6.1, the **Internet Accounts dialogue box** opens.

4 Select **Add**, then you will be prompted to choose what type of account you would like to add.

5 Select **E-mail Account** and then click on **Next.**

6 On the screen that appears, enter the name that you would like to have displayed on your e-mail account. This name will also appear in the header of the messages that you send. After you've typed your display name, click on **Next.**

7 On the screen that appears, enter your e-mail address in the text box provided and click on **Next.**

> ## Important
>
> Windows Mail is an e-mail program, not an ISP. You must have an active e-mail account with an ISP to use Windows Mail.

8 On the next screen, you are prompted to enter your e-mail account settings information. Your ISP will supply you with these settings. Enter these settings and click on **Next.**

9 On the **Internet Mail Logon screen**, enter the user name and password for your e-mail account. Make sure that you select the **Remember password option**, then click on **Next.**

10 The final screen is a confirmation screen. You can choose to download your mail immediately or wait. When you've made your selection, click on **Finish.** You're returned to the **Internet Accounts dialogue box**.

11 Click on **Close**, the dialogue box closes and you're taken back to the Windows Mail user interface.

Now your mail account should be set up and ready to use.

Managing Mail Accounts

Once you've set up an e-mail account, you may find that you need to change or delete it. You can do that by returning to the same menu that you used to set up the account.

1 Open **Windows Mail**.

2 Go to **Tools > Accounts**.

3 In the **Internet Accounts dialogue box** that appears, highlight the account that you want to change or remove.

4 If you want to remove the account, click on the **Remove button**.

5 You will be prompted to confirm your decision to remove the account. Click on **Yes** and the account will be removed from your listing.

6 If you want to make changes to the account, click on the **Properties button**. This takes you to the **Account Properties dialogue box** shown in Figure 6.2, where you can make the necessary changes.

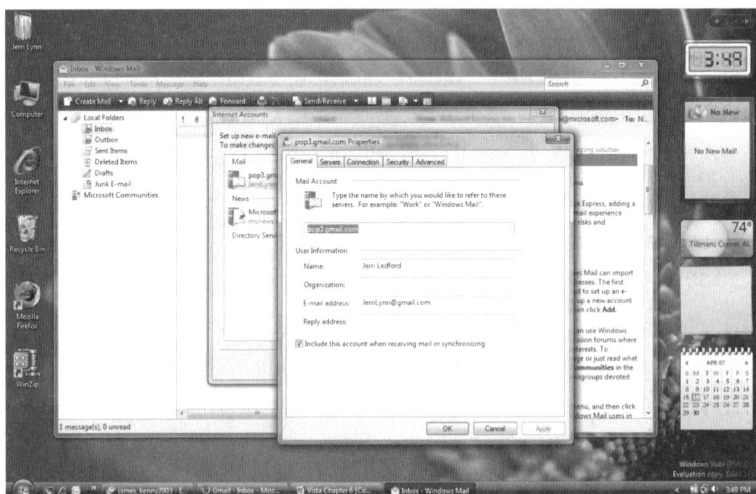

Figure 6.2
Use the Account Properties dialogue box to make changes to your e-mail account.

7 When you have finished making changes, click on **Apply** and then click on **OK** to be returned to the **Internet Accounts dialogue box**.

8 If you've finished making changes, click on **Close** to be returned to **Windows Mail**.

→ Customising Windows Mail

If you've ever seen an e-mail message that contains a signature at the bottom of the message or has been sent on electronic stationery, then you've seen messages that come from a customised mailbox. You can customise your mailbox, too, to reflect your personal tastes and working habits.

To begin customising your mailbox, go to **Tools > Options.** The **Options dialogue box** appears, as shown in Figure 6.3.

The Options dialogue box contains tabs that allow you to make changes to a number of different aspects of Windows Mail.

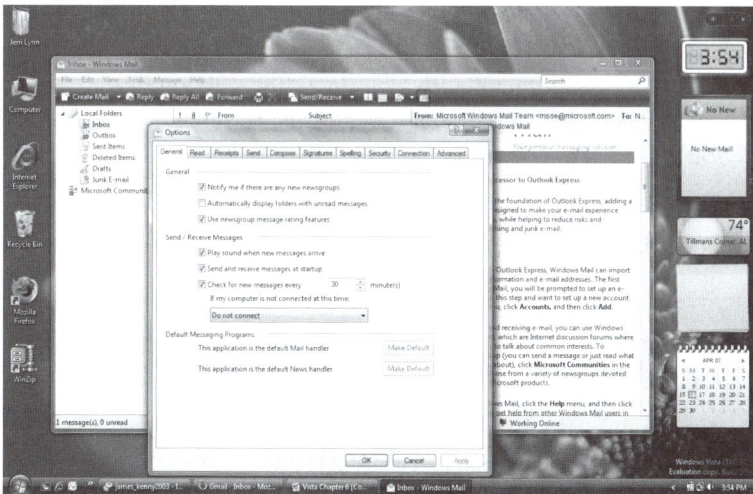

Figure 6.3
The Options dialogue box is where you can customise your Windows Mail.

- **General**—The General tab contains general options for the way Windows Mail behaves when new messages arrive, how often the program checks for new messages and how newsgroup (RSS feed) messages are handled. There is also an option on this tab to make Windows Mail your default e-mail program.

- **Read**—The Read tab contains options for how messages behave when they are read. There are also options here for how newsgroup items are handled and font settings.

- **Receipts**—A receipt is a confirmation that you have read a message that someone else has sent you or that someone else has read a message that you have sent them. The Receipts tab allows you to change those settings to suit your personal preferences.

- **Send**—The Send tab controls how your messages and e-mail program behave when you send messages. Use the options on this tab to choose settings such as including the original message with replies or saving a copy of a sent message in the Sent file. There are also options on this tab that control the format in which you receive e-mail and newsgroup postings.

- **Compose**—The Compose tab is where you set the font size for your messages, include electronic stationery features if you would like to use one and set electronic business cards that you would like to include with your messages.

- **Signatures**—Signatures are common on business e-mails these days.

Jargon buster

A **signature** is a short block of text that includes your name and contact or other information. This block of text is automatically attached to every new message that you send out.

The Signatures tab is where you can set up your signature and define how and when that signature appears on your messages.

- **Spelling**—The Spelling tab is where you set the behaviour of the application that checks the spelling in messages that you send out.

- **Security**—Security is a major concern and one of the improved features in Windows Mail is the security capabilities that are available to you. Use this tab to set how your messages are handled if they are possibly suspicious, how attachments are handled and to manage other security settings that are designed to protect you.

- **Connection**—Not everyone is on an always-on broadband connection. However, even people who are offline sometimes want to work in their mailbox. This tab allows you to set how and when your system will connect to the Internet when you're working in your e-mail box.

- **Advanced**—The Advanced settings tab contains advanced options for mail handling, such as how contacts and message threads are handled. There is also an option here to maintain the way that messages are stored in your Windows Mail program.

→ Navigating the Windows Mail Interface

The Windows Mail interface is fairly intuitive to use. It is similar in layout to Outlook and Outlook Express, so if you've ever used either of those programs in the past, you should be able to acclimatise to Windows Mail very quickly.

The program is set up with standard toolbar and command buttons across the top of the page, as you can see in Figure 6.4.

The options and buttons there allow you to manage your e-mail box, send, receive, reply to and forward mail. There are also

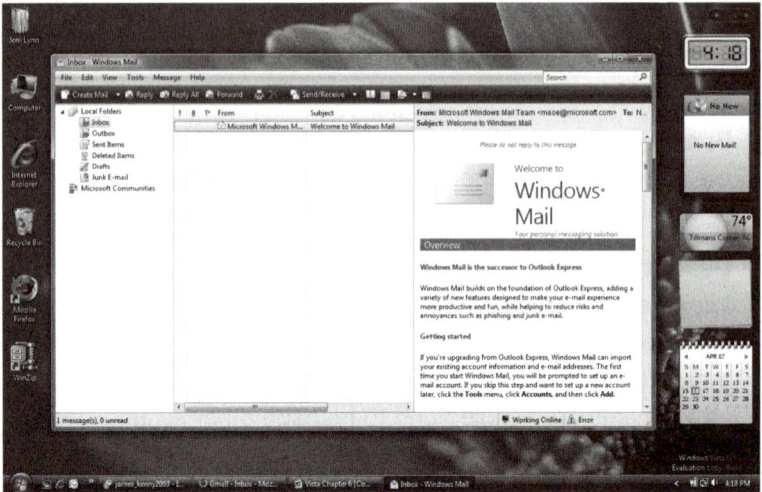

Figure 6.4
The Windows Mail interface is intuitive and easy to use.

options to print and change the way you view the different features of the program.

Below those toolbars are three columns. The column to the left is your Folder view. The highlighted folder is the one in which you are working at the time.

The centre column lists the messages that you have received. Messages that have been read appear in a normal font, while new messages appear in a bold font.

The column on the far right is your Reading pane. This is where the contents of the highlighted message are displayed.

Changing Your Windows Mail View

It is also possible for you to change the way that your mail appears to you in your inbox. To change your Windows Mail view, do the following.

1 Open **Windows Mail**.

2 Go to **View** and highlight **Current View**, as shown in Figure 6.5.

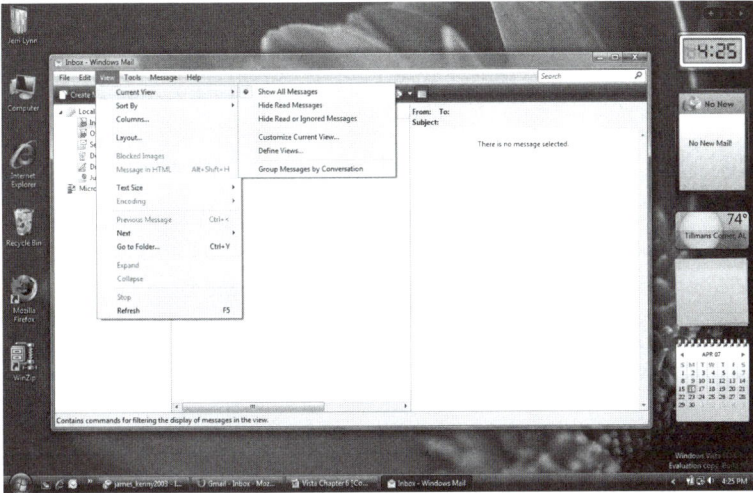

Figure 6.5
Change your view of messages to meet your needs.

3 The options available in the **Current View** menu include (see Figure 6.5) Show All Messages, Hide Read Messages, Hide Read or Ignored Messages, Customize Current View and Define Views. You also have the option to Group Messages by Conversation instead of by date. When you make a selection, it goes into effect immediately and you're returned to Windows Mail.

→ Handling Messages Effectively

E-mail has become one of the most used methods of communication. In fact, some organisations receive so many e-mails that if they were not delivered for some reason, they would effectively grind to a halt. Even at home, these days we rely heavily on e-mail for communication with family and friends. When you rely on your e-mail, you need to be able to handle the messages as effectively as possible.

Sending and Receiving Mail

Sending an e-mail requires that you first create one. To create a message, you take the following steps.

1 Click on the **Create Mail** button on the Windows Mail interface.

2 A new, blank e-mail appears. Add the e-mail address to which you want to send the message in the box.

3 Type a subject for your message.

4 Then type the message in the body of the message.

5 When you've finished, click on **Send** to send the message.

Windows Mail will send the message immediately if you are connected to the Internet. If you are not connected to the Internet, the message is stored in your outbox until the next time you connect to the Internet and send and receive e-mail.

Windows Mail is set up to automatically send and receive e-mail every half hour. You can change that setting by going to **Tools > Options** and the frequency with which the program checks your mail is given on the **General tab**. When you've made the change, click on **Apply** and then click on **OK** to return to Windows Mail.

You can also send and receive e-mails even when you're not scheduled to by clicking on the **Send and Receive button**. There is also a **Send and Receive menu** beside that button, which allows you to just send or just receive.

Sending and Receiving Attachments

Jargon buster

Attachments are any files that are attached to e-mails.

To open an attachment, do the following.

1 Click on the message to which the file is attached.

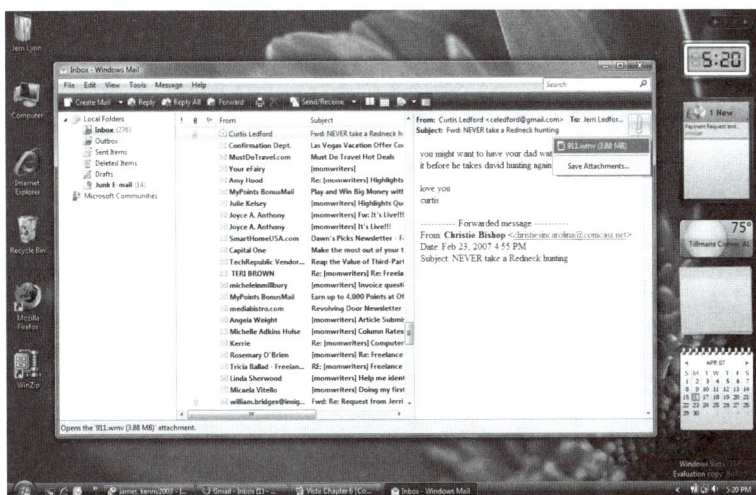

Figure 6.6
Attachments are indicated by a paperclip icon.

2 The message opens in the Reading pane and you'll see a paperclip in the upper right corner, as shown in Figure 6.6. Click on the paperclip and then click on the name of the file that appears and it will open.

3 If you prefer to download the file to your computer, click on **Save Attachments** instead.

4 In the **Save Attachments dialogue box**, select the location you want the file saved to and click on **Save.**

Sorting and Filing Messages

With the volume of e-mails that most people receive, some method of sorting and filing it is necessary. Sorting it is easy with Windows Mail. Open Windows Mail, then, as shown in Figure 6.7, click on **View > Sort By** and select how you want your messages sorted. You can always change the way your messages are sorted again if it turns out that the method chosen doesn't work for you.

To file your messages, you first need folders in which to file them. To create a folder, right-click on the **Inbox** and select **New Folder** from the menu that appears. A dialogue box opens in

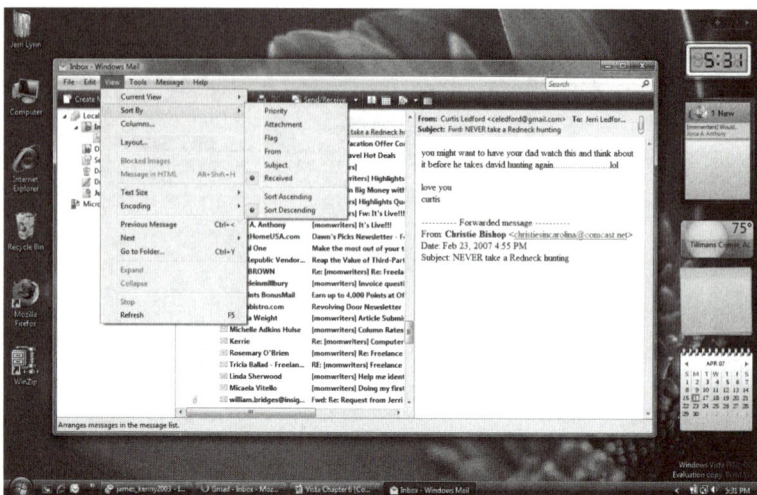

Figure 6.7
Choose the sorting method that suits your needs.

which you can type the name of the file, then click on **OK.** You can repeat this process to create as many files as you need.

Once you have your files in place, you can click on and drag your messages into the appropriate files. Alternatively, you can right-click on the message and select **Send to Folder** from the menu that appears. The **Move dialogue box** then appears. Select the folder you want the message moved to, then click on **OK.**

Creating Message Rules

Jargon buster

Message rules are the guidelines by means of which you can automatically sort or handle some or all of your messages.

In Windows Mail, you can set up message rules for incoming mail in just a few minutes. Here's how.

1 Open **Windows Mail**.

2 Go to **Tools**.

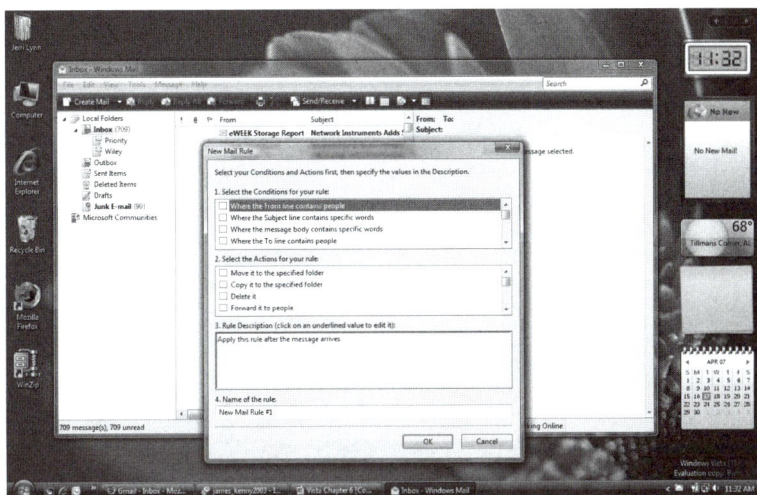

Figure 6.8
Use the New Mail Rule dialogue box to create your first mail rule.

3 Highlight **Message Rules** and then select **Mail.** The
Message Rules dialogue box appears. If you have never
created a message rule before, the dialogue box will open
the **New Main Rule dialogue box**, as shown in Figure 6.8.
If, however, you have created message rules already, then
the dialogue box opens to the **Mail Rules tab**, as shown in
Figure 6.9.

4 If you're creating a rule for the first time, use the **New Mail
Rule dialogue box** to create your first rule by selecting first
the *conditions* for the rule.

5 Then select the *actions* for the rule.

6 In the third section of the dialogue box, you'll see your
conditions and actions displayed. If there are elements of the
conditions and actions that can be further customised, those
elements are blue links to further customisation, as shown in
Figure 6.10.

7 Finally, enter a name for the rule you've created in the text
box provided, though you can leave the name that is there if
you prefer.

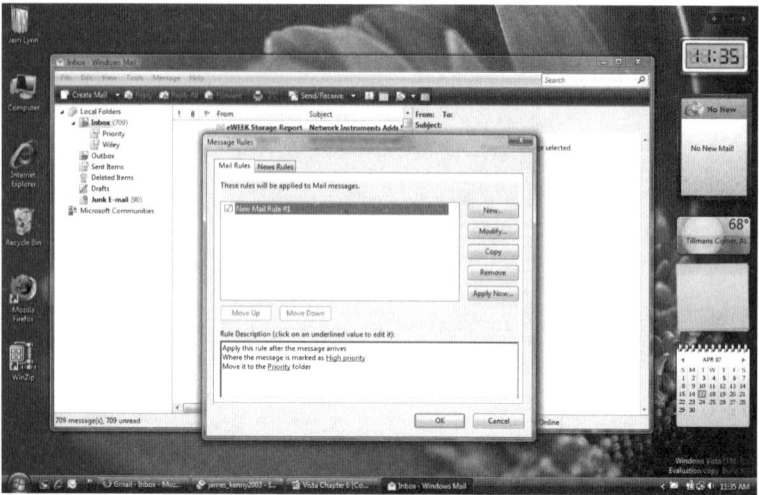

Figure 6.9
Existing rules are managed from the Mail Rules tab.

8 When you've finished, click on **OK** and the rule will have
been created. You're taken to the **Message Rules dialogue
box** where you click **OK** again to close it.

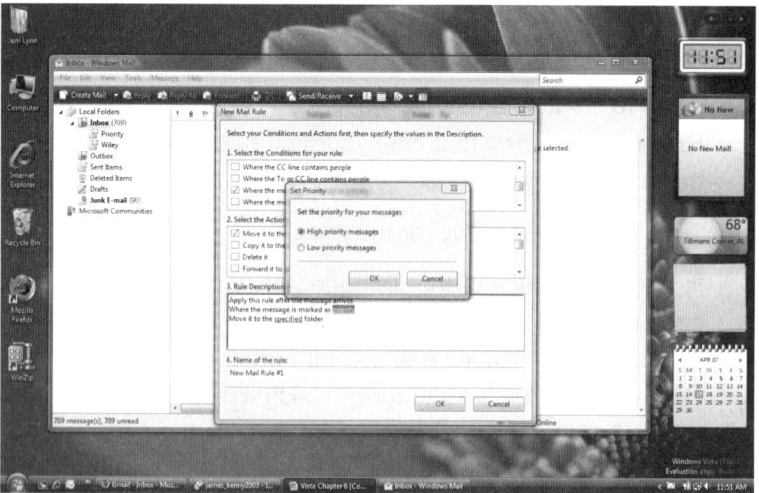

Figure 6.10
Click on the blue links to add further detail to your message rule.

Managing and Deleting Rules

Later, having created rules for your messages, you may find that you need to change or even delete those rules.

Here's how to **change** a rule.

1 Open **Windows Mail**.

2 Go to **Tools > Message Rules > Mail**. The **Message Rules dialogue box** appears.

3 In the dialogue box is a list of existing rules. Click on the rule that you want to change, then click on **Modify**.

4 The **Edit Mail Rule dialogue box** appears. Make your changes and click on **OK** to return to the **Message Rules dialogue box**.

5 When you've finished editing your rules, click on **OK** again to save the changes and close the dialogue box.

If what you really want is to **delete** a rule (or multiple rules), go to **Tools > Message Rules > Mail** and, when the **Message Rules dialogue box** appears, click on the **Mail Rules tab**. Then, highlight the message that you want to delete and click on **Remove.** You'll be prompted to confirm your decision. Click on **Yes** and you'll be returned to the **Message Rules dialogue box**. Click on **OK** to save your changes and close the dialogue box.

→ Using the Address Book

The address book in Windows Mail isn't quite as easy to find as it is in Outlook or Outlook Express, but it's still there, right along the toolbar at the top of the Windows Mail interface. The icon looks like a small address book. Click on that icon and your address book opens, as shown in Figure 6.11.

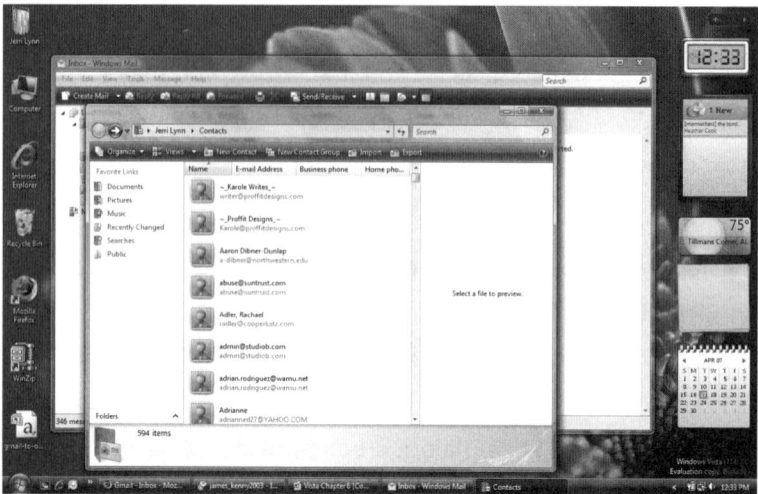

Figure 6.11
Your address book is where all of your contacts' information is stored.

Finding Contacts

All of the contacts in your address book are arranged in alphabetical order. So, if you want to find a particular one, you can scroll to the letter that starts his or her name and find it.

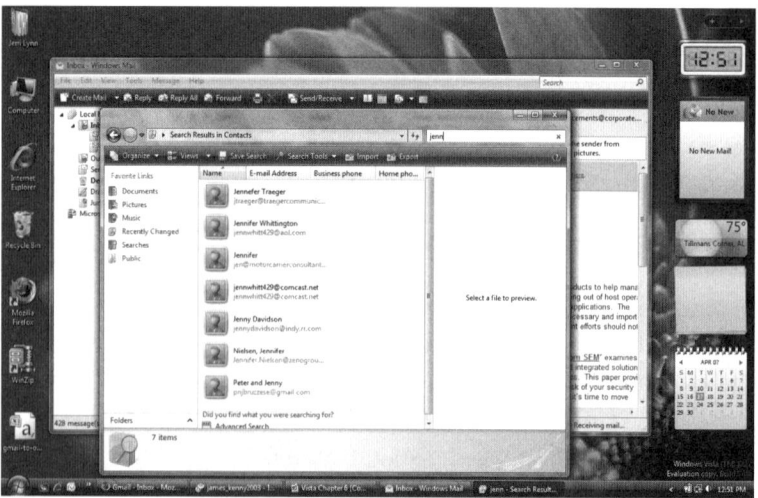

Figure 6.12
Type a name in the search box to locate a contact.

Another way to arrange your contacts is in reverse alphabetical order. To do that, click on the **Name heading** above your contacts' names.

Another way to find a contact is to type the name you are looking for in the search bar to the right of the address bar. As you type, your contacts' list is searched for matching names, as shown in Figure 6.12.

Adding Contacts

Adding a contact to your address book is a quick task.

1 Open your address book.

2 Select **New Contact** from the **address book toolbar**. A **Properties dialogue box** appears.

3 Type your new contact's information in the fields provided, as shown in Figure 6.13.

4 Additional information can be added according to the tab under which that information falls. Tabs include Name and E-mail, Home, Work, Family, Notes and IDs.

Figure 6.13
The Properties dialogue box is where you enter your contact's information.

5 When you have finished entering all the contact information you want to include, click on **OK** and you are returned to the **Contacts screen**.

Automatic Additions

There is one more little trick that you should know about Windows Mail. It's how to have all of the contacts to whom you send a reply e-mail automatically added to your address book. To enable automatic additions, follow these steps.

1 Open **Windows Mail**.

2 Go to **Tools > Options**. The **Options dialogue box** opens.

3 Click on the **Send** tab.

4 Select the option that reads **Automatically put people I reply to in my Contacts list**.

5 Click on **Apply** and then click on **OK** to return to the **Contacts screen**.

7

Creating a Home Network

In this lesson you'll be introduced to Windows Networking, LANs, Internet Connection Sharing and Wireless Networks.

→ Understanding Windows Networking

Networking. There's a word that will scare even the savviest of computer users. It's not because networks are all that difficult to create, now, but they used to be.

In the past, creating a network was a bit of a nightmare. Today, Windows makes it much easier to both create and use a network. Before you get started, though, there are a few things that you should understand.

Understanding LANs

When you hear the term network, you may also hear a phrase like "local area network" or its acronym, LAN.

Jargon buster

A **LAN** is a type of network that connects computers together locally. For example, when you network together the computers in your house, you're creating a LAN. The Internet is what's called a **wide area network** (**WAN**). It covers a great distance.

LANs can either be wired – meaning the computers in the network are connected by wires or cables – or they can be wireless, which – you guessed it – means that there are no cables or wires connecting the computers.

A wired network is created by connecting Ethernet-enabled computers to a network router with Ethernet cables. Ethernet cables are those cables that look like a larger version of a phone line. You may have heard them called Cat 5 cables or even RJ-45 cables. Wired networks are great, but they are limited by the cables.

An alternative to a wired network is a wireless network. In a wireless network, computers are connected via network interface cards (NICs). Because the computers can communicate using the NICs, there is no need to have a router to connect them. However, if you plan to share an Internet connection between the computers, then you may want to have a wireless broadband router, which will enable all of the computers in your network to connect to your single broadband Internet connection.

Important

Allowing all of your computers to use a dial-up Internet connection via a wireless network isn't possible. Because the dial-up connection is slow, and must be accomplished through a telephone line, it only creates additional headaches. If you want all of the computers on your wireless network to share the same Internet connection, you must be using cable or DSL broadband Internet.

The NICs that computers use to connect to a wireless network communicate using a common language – called a protocol. The protocol that wireless networking devices use is called the Wireless Networking Standard, which you'll often hear referred to as 802.11a or b or g.

Most wireless networking equipment today is 802.11b or 802.11g. The main difference between the two is speed – 802.11g being the faster of the two. However, you can use both 802.11b and 802.11g equipment on the same network. The thing to keep in mind is that it is the slower protocol (802.11b) that will determine how fast your network is.

Now, the question is, is the difference in speed really that noticeable? It depends. Some people will notice the difference, others will not. For the best results, though, we recommend that you use 802.11g equipment whenever possible.

→ Planning Your Network

All of this may seem very confusing, but, when you begin to plan your network, you'll quickly learn that it's not that confusing really. The first decision that you need to make is what kind of network you want: wired or wireless?

A wired network requires a network router (or hub) and enough ethernet cable to connect all of the computers that you want to include in the network to the router. Also, each of the computers must have an ethernet port.

A wireless network requires a wireless router and each of the computers in the network will need an NIC. Most computers today come with wireless capabilities built in, but if yours doesn't have pre-existing wireless capabilities, you can install NICs easily and inexpensively.

In either case, if you're going to be sharing the Internet, you'll need a broadband Internet router.

Once you have the equipment, you should install it according to the manufacturer's directions. Because there are so many different varieties of equipment on the market, it's impossible to provide directions for installation for everyone here. However, your equipment will come with instructions that should be fairly easy to follow. In fact, most equipment these days comes with very detailed, step-by-step instructions and some of it even comes with digital tutorials that walk you through the process.

→ Understanding Internet Connection Sharing

After you've connected your network, it's time to begin creating the actual software connections. Before you get too deep into that, however, you should really understand what Internet connection sharing (ICS) is.

ICS is what most home networks are. Each is a network of computers that are connected solely for the purpose of sharing an Internet connection. In most cases, the network is a wireless one and the Internet is the only shared component. It is possible to add other shared components, but most people don't.

To set up an ICS network, you must first set up your ICS host.

7

1 Go to **Start > Control Panel > Network and Internet > Network and Sharing Center**. The **Network and Sharing Center dialogue box** shown in Figure 7.1 opens.

2 Select **Manage network connections** from the menu on the left. The **Network Connections dialogue box** opens, displaying a list of the available network connections for your computer, as shown in Figure 7.2.

3 Right-click on the Internet connection icon and select **Properties**. The **Local Area Connection Properties dialogue box** appears.

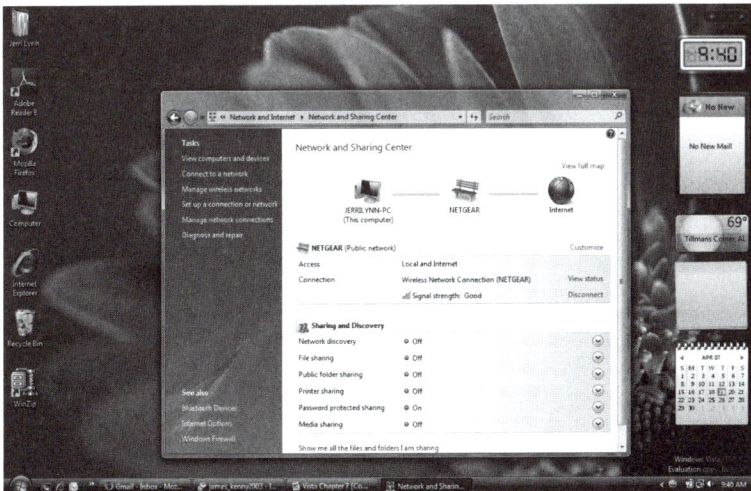

Figure 7.1
Manage your network using the Network and Sharing Center.

Figure 7.2
View available network connections in the Network Connections
dialogue box.

4 Click on the **Sharing tab**.

5 On the **Sharing tab**, select **Allow other network users to connect through this computer's Internet connection**.

6 Click on **OK** and you are returned to the **Network Connections dialogue box**.

7 Close all the open windows and then your ICS host setup will be complete.

Once the ICS host has been set up, then you can configure other computers on the network to share that Internet connection.

Important

You will have to configure every computer that's connected to your network to share the Internet via the ICS host. Repeat the steps below for each computer.

1 Make sure that the ICS host (the computer you set up above) is online. Keep that Internet connection active during the following process.

2 On the first computer that will be sharing with the ICS host, go to **Start > Internet Explorer**.

3 In Internet Explorer, select **Tools > Internet Options.** The **Internet Options dialogue box** (shown in Figure 7.3) opens.

4 Select the **Connections** tab.

5 Select **LAN Settings.** The **LAN Settings dialogue box** appears, as shown in Figure 7.4.

6 Make sure that all of the selections shown in the dialogue box are deselected (that is, there are no ticks in the boxes).

7 Click on **OK** in all of the open dialogue boxes to save your settings and return to Internet Explorer.

8 Now go to **Start > Control Panel > Network and Internet > Network and Sharing Center.**

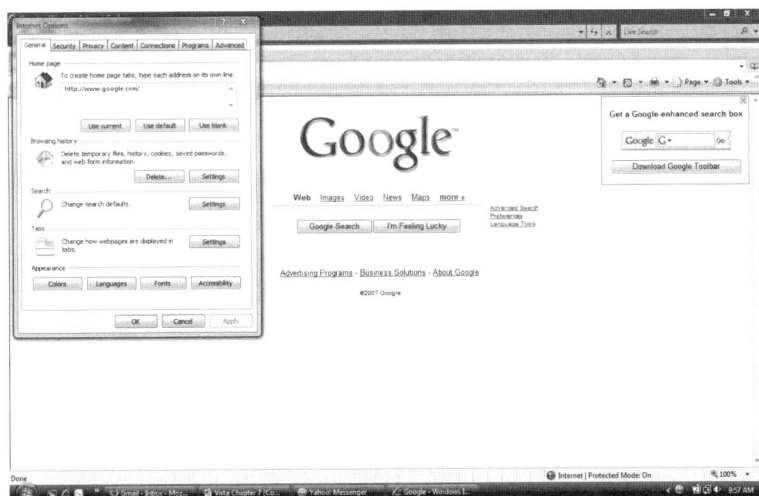

Figure 7.3
The Internet Options dialogue box.

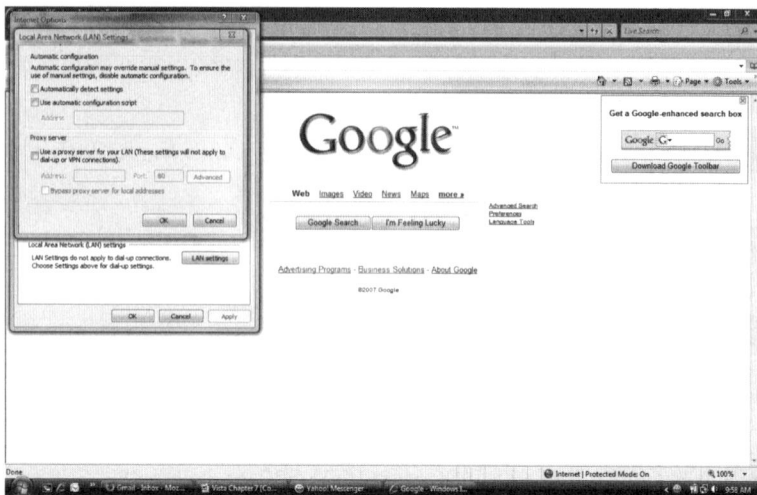

Figure 7.4
Use the LAN Settings dialogue box to ensure that you can share the
Internet connection.

> # Important
>
> To make these changes to your network and sharing options, you must
> be signed into Vista on an administrator's profile. If you are not logged
> into the administrator's profile, log into it before attempting to make
> these changes.

9 In the **Sharing and Discovery section** of the **Network
and Sharing dialogue box**, make sure that all of your
network and sharing options are turned on, as shown in
Figure 7.5.

10 Close all open dialogue boxes to return to Internet
Explorer.

You should now be able to access the Internet connection via
your Internet Explorer browser.

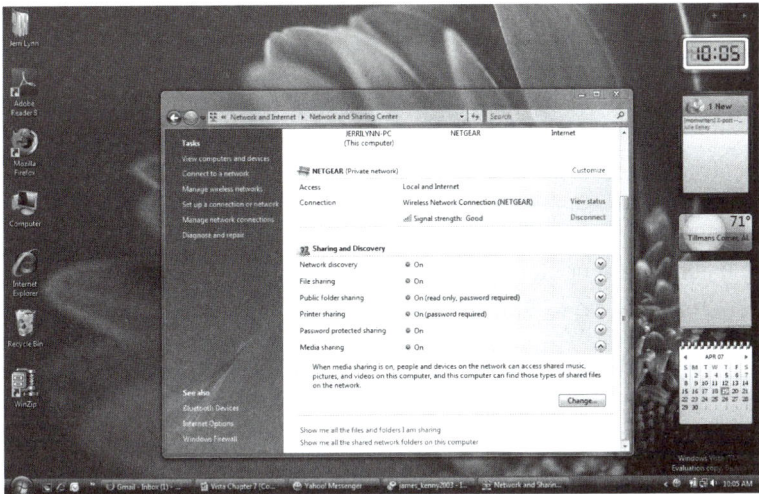

Figure 7.5
Turn on all network and sharing options to share the Internet
connection.

Important

If you're using a different browser, such as Firefox or Netscape, your
setup procedure might differ slightly from the steps listed above. If you
are using a different browser, the help documentation for that browser
should include instructions for sharing the Internet connection.

→ Setting Up a Wireless Network

A wireless network is a little easier to set up than the ICS
connection above. First, make sure that your wireless router is
installed according to the manufacturer's instructions. Also, make
sure that a wireless network adapter is installed in every
computer that will access your wireless network. Then, follow the
steps below to create the wireless connection.

1 On the computer that you're trying to connect to the wireless
network, go to **Start > Control Panel > Network and Internet.**

2 Click on the **View network status link**, below **Network and
Sharing Center**. The **Network and Sharing Center
dialogue box** appears.

3 In the menu on the left, click on **Connect to a network**. As
shown in Figure 7.6, the **Connect to a network dialogue
box** appears.

4 Select the network to which you would like to connect. If the
network you are connecting to is unsecured, you will be
prompted to confirm that you want to connect to an
unsecured network. Click on **Yes** to connect. If the network

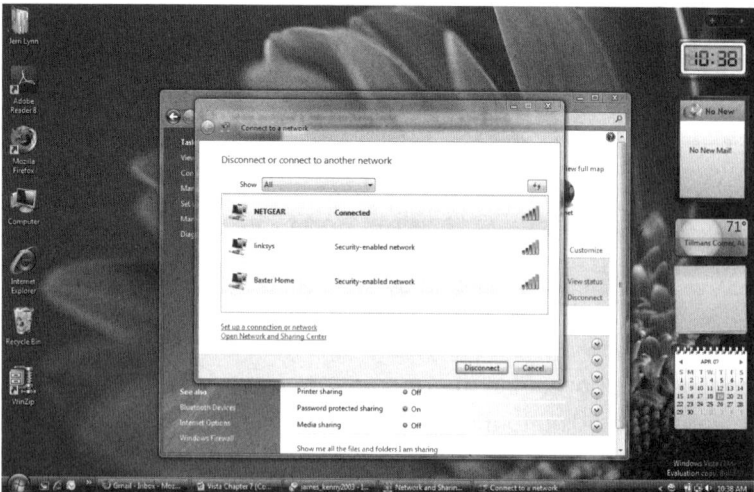

Figure 7.6
Select the network to which you would like to connect.

has been secured, then you will be prompted to enter the security password or 26-digit key before you connect. Once you've entered the information, click on **OK.**

5 You should now be connected to the network.

→ Sharing Files and Printers

Once you've set your computer up in a network, then you might like to share files and printers between the computers in that network. Sharing files and printers is a little more difficult than just sharing Internet connections, but you can create a sharing situation without the help of a computer professional.

7

Important

Use caution when creating a sharing situation. When you're sharing files and printers in a network, the other people in the network will have access to those files. That means your personal information could be at risk if you don't take proper security precautions.

Before you try to set up a sharing situation in your network, make sure that sharing is enabled on your computer. If you followed the instructions under "Understanding Internet Connection Sharing" earlier in this chapter, your sharing capabilities should already be active.

When you're ready to enable file and printer sharing, follow these steps.

Important

You must follow these instructions on all of the computers from which you would like to enable file and print sharing.

---

1 Go to **Start > Control Panel** and click on the **View Network Status and Tasks link**, below **Network and Internet**.

2 When the **Network and Sharing Center dialogue box** appears, select the **Customize link**, on the right of the page beneath your network diagram. As shown in Figure 7.7, the **Set Network Location dialogue box** appears.

3 Under **Customize network settings**, type the network name for your computer. Note that the network name should be the same for all the computers in the network and it's usually best to leave it as the default name provided by Vista.

4 Next, click on the **Private option** to make your network private – that is, not available to the general public. Then click on **Next**.

5 The next screen confirms your settings. If they are correct, click on **Close**.

Now you are ready to enable your printer and file-sharing capabilities. Here's how you enable printer sharing.

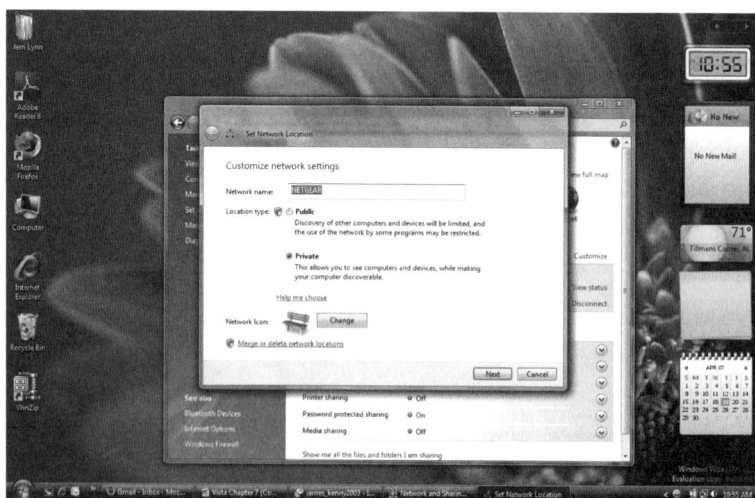

Figure 7.7
Use the Set Network Location dialogue box to customise your network settings.

1 First, make sure that your printer is turned on. Then, on the computer to which the printer is connected, go to **Start > Control Panel** and click on the **Printer link**, below **Hardware and Sound.**

2 Right-click on the icon that represents the printer you want to share and select **Sharing**. The **Printer Properties dialogue box** appears.

3 Click on the **Sharing tab** and then select **Change Sharing Options.**

4 Select the option to share the printer.

5 Type a name for the printer in the **Share Name box**.

6 Place a tick next to **Render print jobs on client computers**, as shown in Figure 7.8.

7 Then click on **Apply** and **OK** to close the **Printer Properties dialogue box**. Your printer should now be ready to share.

Next, you need to enable the sharing of files. There are actually two ways to share your files in Vista and here's one of them.

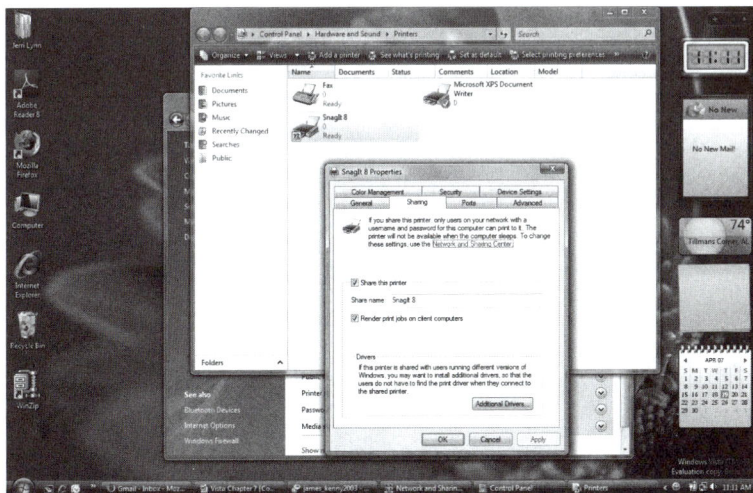

Figure 7.8
You can enable printer sharing in the Printer Properties dialogue box.

1 On the computer that has the files you want to share, go to **Start > Computer.** The **Computer dialogue box** opens.

2 On the left side of the dialogue box is a Navigation pane. Click on **Folders** in that pane to expand your list of available folders.

3 Next, click on the **Public folder**. This folder (shown in Figure 7.9) is where you can place documents to make them publically available to other users in the network.

4 To add a document or file to the folders listed there, simply drag them from their current location on to the desired folder. Once there, your files are available to everyone on the network.

You can also share files and folders on your computer with only certain other users in a network. To share selectively, follow these steps.

1 To share a document or file with only certain users, first navigate to the location of that document or file on your hard drive.

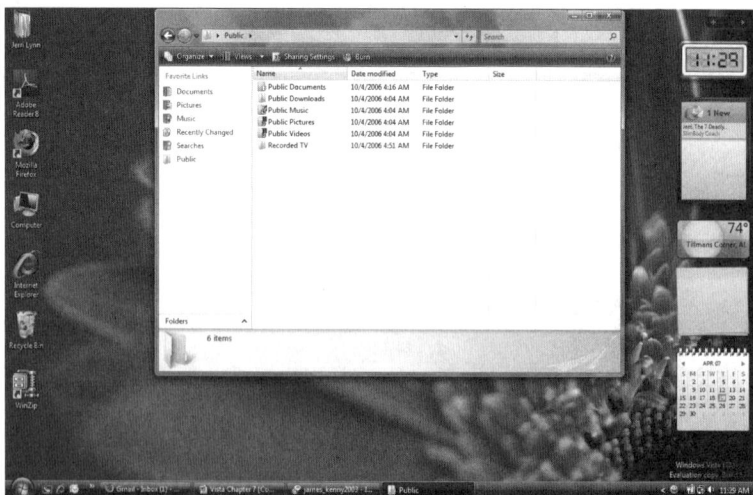

Figure 7.9
The Public folder allows you to share files with all users in a network.

2 Right-click on the document or file and select **Share**, as shown in Figure 7.10.

3 The **File Sharing dialogue box** appears. In the dropdown menu in that dialogue box, select the person (or people) you would like to share the file or document with.

4 Click on **Add.** The person you have selected will appear in the list below the dropdown menu.

5 Next, you should set permissions for that person. To do that, click on the **Permission Level dropdown menu**, next to the user's name, as shown in Figure 7.11.

6 Select the permission level that you would like to allow that user. You have three options: Reader, Contributor and Co-owner. Readers can only read the document or file. Contributors can make changes to the document or file, but only owners and co-owners can delete a document or file.

7 When you've finished, click on **Share.** You will be prompted to confirm your decision. Click on **Yes** and you'll be returned to the **File Sharing dialogue box**.

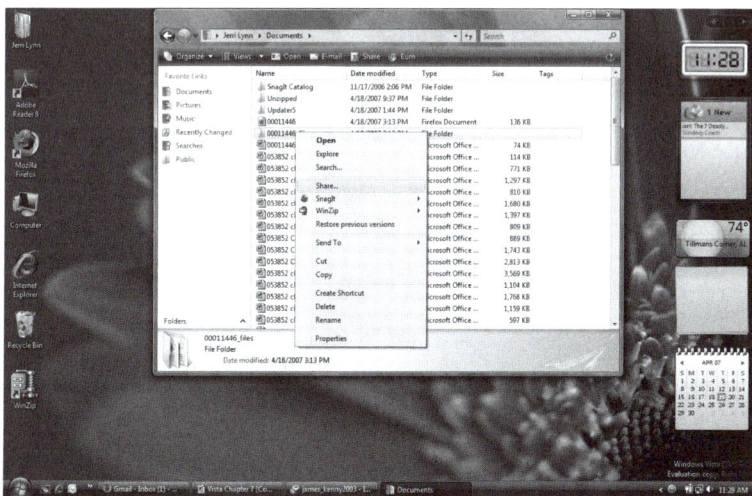

Figure 7.10
Right-click on a document or folder to find the Share option.

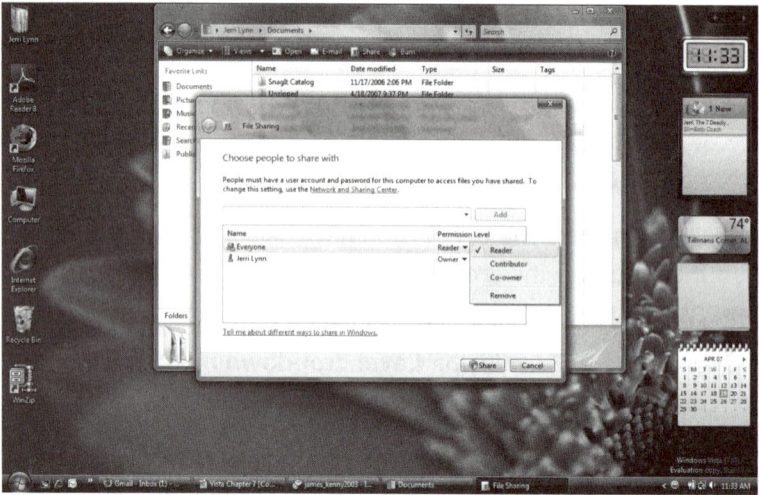

Figure 7.11
Set the permission level for the users you allow to share your files.

8 The **File Sharing dialogue box** will show the file being shared and, once that action has been completed, you'll see a confirmation like the one shown in Figure 7.12. Click on

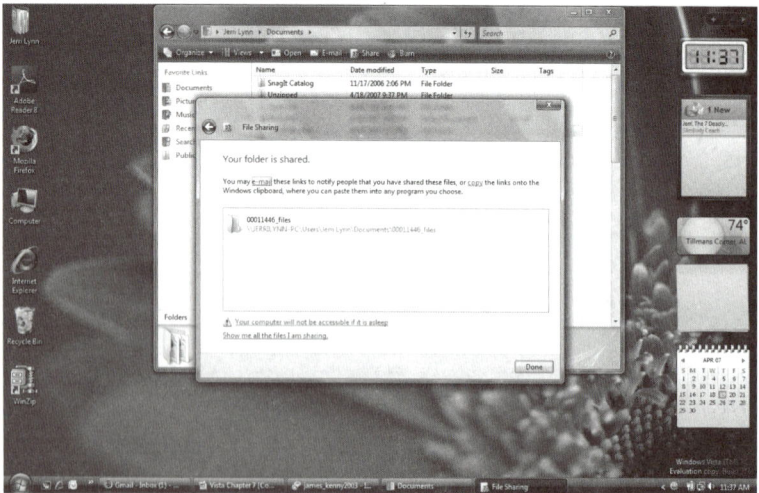

Figure 7.12
When a file is shared properly, a confirmation appears.

Done and you'll be returned to the location of your file on your computer's hard drive.

You are now sharing only the selected file with only the selected users. At any time when you don't want to share with a user any more, you can go back to that menu and, in the **Permissions menu**, select **Remove** to remove the user from the list of people with whom you are sharing.

8

Managing User Accounts

In this lesson you'll learn how to create and manage User Accounts.

→ Understanding User Accounts

Having user accounts is how you can organise for different people to have different profiles on your computer. These different profiles allow you to set permissions for things, such as installing programs, and keep personal or private information away from other users.

There are four types of user accounts in Windows Vista.

- **The administrator account**—The administrator account is a built-in account that is usually hidden away from the logon screen. This account is the one that has unlimited privileges on your computer. Whoever has access to the administrator account can install and uninstall software or make any changes to the operating system that they want. It's a good idea to keep this account hidden and password protected from all other users.

- **The user account (with administrator privileges)**—This account is similar to the administrator account, but it's not exactly the same. Someone who has a user account with administrator privileges can install and uninstall software and make changes to most settings on the computer. However, there are some security measures in place to ensure that the person using this account doesn't overstep his or her bounds and damage the operating system or other users' accounts.

- **Standard user accounts**—A standard user account has enough privileges to make it possible for its user to work as you normally would. This means that you can work in programs and applications and change some customisation settings. However, this account does not have enough privileges to enable its user to make changes that will affect other users and override parental controls.

- **Guest accounts**—These accounts are designed to allow guests – people who don't normally use your computer – to have access to it. With a guest account, you can set privilege levels so that the guest user can only surf the net, check e-mails and use installed programs. That's where guest users' privileges end, however. Guests cannot make any changes to any of the settings or programs on the computer.

When setting up your computer, you should probably only include one administrator account (aside from the built-in administrator's account). Having only one administrator account ensures that other users don't accidentally make changes that can harm your computer.

→ Creating and Managing User Accounts

8

User accounts can only be created and managed from the administrator's profile on the computer. To create a user account, follow these steps.

1 Go to **Start > Control Panel > User Accounts and Family Safety**. The **User Accounts dialogue box** opens.

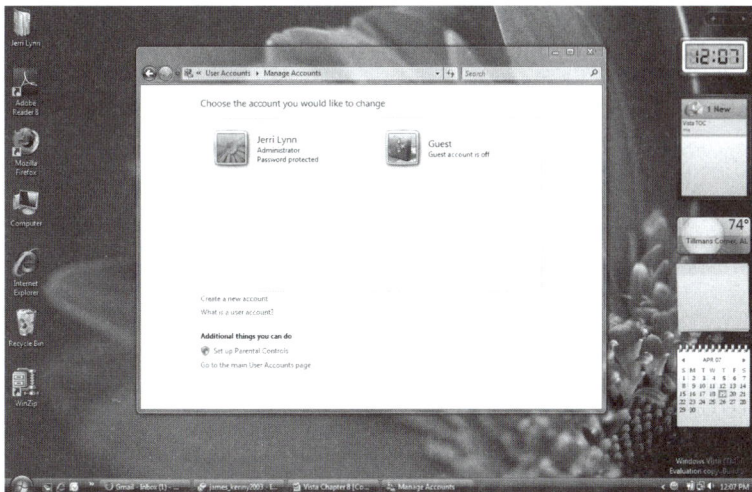

Figure 8.1
Use the Manage Accounts dialogue box to create and manage accounts.

2 Under **User Accounts**, select the **Add or Remove Accounts link**. The **Manage Accounts dialogue box** appears, as shown in Figure 8.1.

3 Click on the **Create a new account link**.

4 On the screen that appears, enter the account name in the text box provided.

5 Select the type of account (administrator or standard user) that you want to create.

6 Click on **Create Account**. You are returned to the **User Accounts dialogue box**.

From time to time, you may need to change the settings or privileges for an account or delete one. Here's how you manage your user accounts.

1 Go to **Start > Control Panel > User Accounts and Family Safety**.

2 Select **User Accounts**. The next screen should read **Make changes to your user account**.

3 Select **Manage another account**. You're taken to the **Manage Accounts dialogue box**.

4 Select the account that you would like to change. The next screen is where you'll find the options that you need to make changes, as shown in Figure 8.2.

5 When you've finished making changes to the desired account, close the **Manage Accounts dialogue box**.

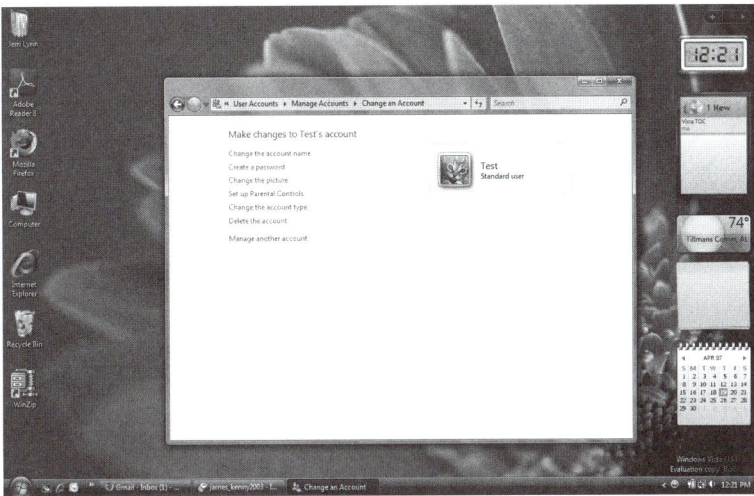

Figure 8.2
Select the option that you would like to change.

9

Using Vista's Multimedia Capabilities

In this lesson you'll learn about playing installed and online games in Vista as well as how to work with digital pictures. You'll also learn about Windows Media Player, AutoPlay and Movie Maker.

→ Playing Games in Vista

The Microsoft Windows Vista operating system is well designed to work with games. Vista comes with a few games, such as Hearts, Solitaire and Freecell, but if you want more than that you will have to buy and install them. Vista includes several game trials, however, that will give you a feel for how games work on it. You can open and play those games once, but will then have to purchase them if you decide you want to keep them on your computer.

Playing Installed Games

To play games that are already installed on your computer, go to the **start menu** and click on **Games**. The menu expands, showing you a list of games available on your computer, as shown in Figure 9.1. Double-click on the game you would like to play to open it.

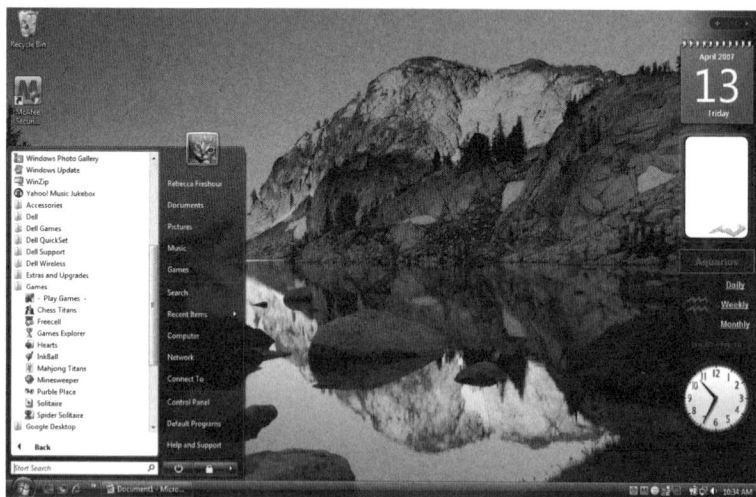

Figure 9.1
The Games menu expands to show its contents.

Playing Online Games

If you would like to go online and play games, a broadband Internet connection is recommended in order to achieve the desired speed.

To play games online, simply connect to the Internet. You can find online games by going to any search engine and typing in' "Internet games". Some games you can play from the website, but some you may have to download and additional drivers to be able to play them. Most of the time, if you like an Internet game you are playing and would like to purchase it, that option is available.

Installing Games

9

If you decide to purchase games for your computer, either from a shop or the Internet, you first need to be sure that the game is compatible with your computer. To check this, read the minimum requirements needed on the label for the game. These should include specifications such as RAM, video card requirements and controllers (when applicable). Also, be sure that the game is compatible with Windows Vista.

Once you have bought a game, most come with an installation CD. Insert the CD into your CD/DVD drive and follow the installation guide, which will take you through the installation process. You can refer to the booklet that comes with the game for other instructions, such as how to play the game, the options the game offers and troubleshooting any issues that may arise while installing the game.

Managing Game Controllers

Game controllers, such as joysticks, are sometimes required to play certain games that you might install on your computer. When purchasing game controllers, be sure that they are compatible with Windows Vista.

To install a game controller, insert the CD-ROM that comes with it (if there is one) and follow the installation instructions. Most controllers now, however, have the "plug and play" feature. All you need to do is insert the cable for the controller into the correct port, then Vista should recognise the device and install it for you.

After the game controllers have been installed on your computer, you can configure the way those controllers are accessed and how they behave by following these steps.

1 Go to **Start > Control Panel > Hardware and Sound**.

2 In the **Hardware and Sound dialogue box**, click on **Game Controllers**. The **Game Controllers dialogue box** appears, as shown in Figure 9.2. Here you should see a list of the controllers that are installed on your computer.

3 Select the device that you want to customise and click on **Properties**.

4 In the dialogue box that appears, make your changes and then click on **OK**.

5 Back in the **Game Controllers dialogue box**, you also have

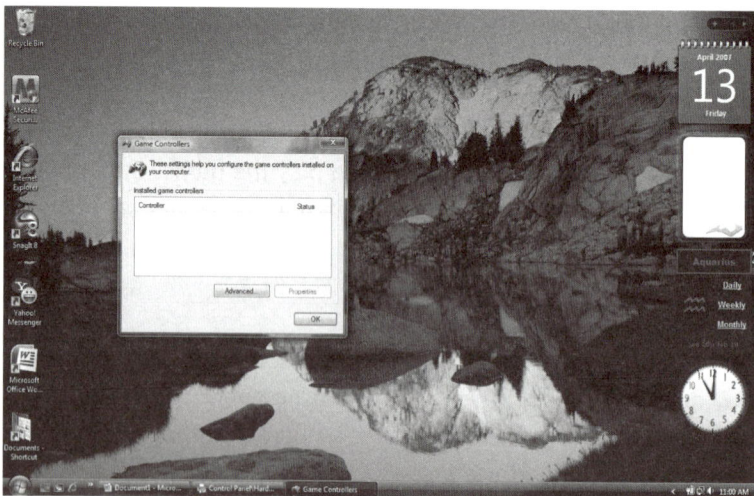

Figure 9.2
The Game Controllers dialogue box.

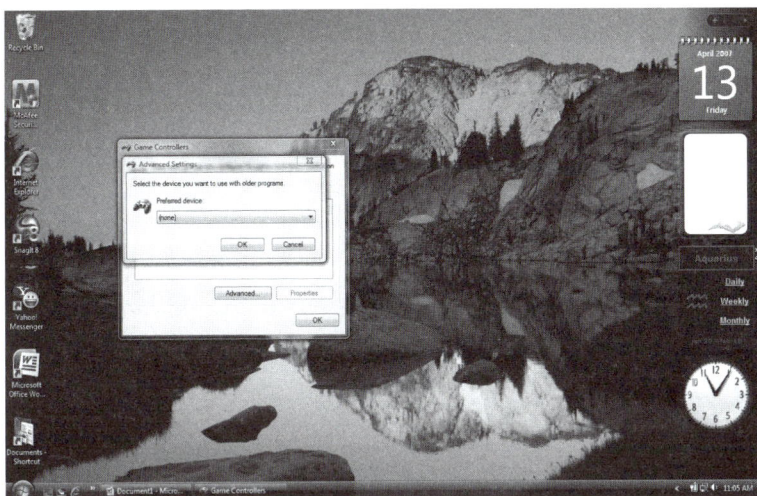

Figure 9.3
The Advanced Settings dialogue box.

an option to change the advanced settings for your controller. To do this, click on **Advanced**.

6 Then, select the device you'd like to change advanced options for, as shown in Figure 9.3. You're taken to the advanced options for that device.

7 Make your changes, then click on **OK**.

8 To close the **Game Controllers dialogue box** and return to your desktop, click on **OK** again.

→ Using the Windows Media Player

With Vista's Windows Media Player, you can play and manage many different types of media, from CDs and DVDs to downloadable multimedia files. According to the features of your computer, you may also be able to rip and burn CDs and DVDs.

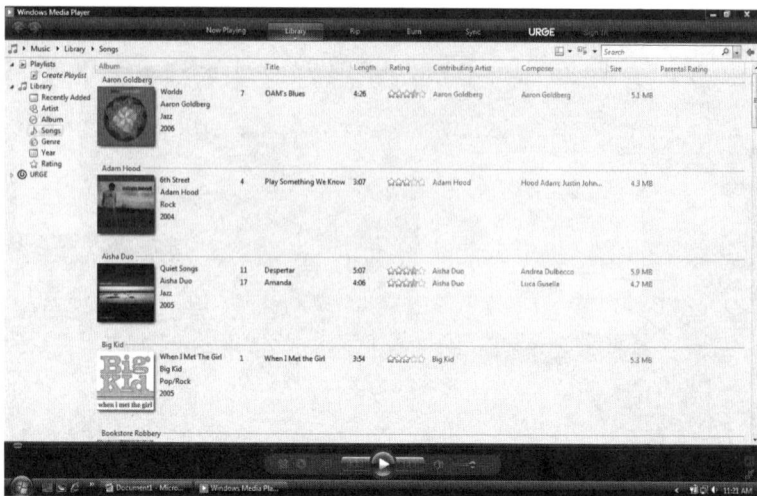

Figure 9.4
The Windows Media Player.

To access the Windows Media Player, go to the **start menu** and
select the **Windows Media Player** icon. This opens the Windows
Media Player, as shown in Figure 9.4.

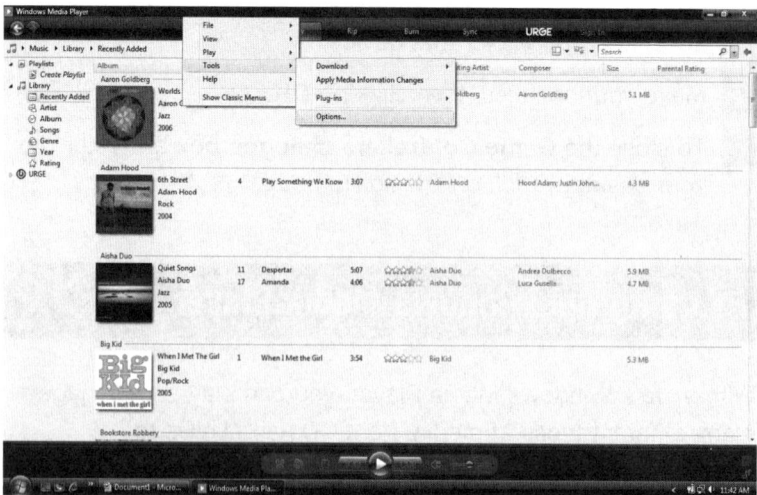

Figure 9.5
Accessing the Options menu.

Configuring the Windows Media Player

You may want to configure the Windows Media Player to meet your specific tastes and needs. To configure it, follow these steps.

1 Right-click on an empty spot in the toolbar.

2 Choose **Tools** from the menu that appears.

3 Then select **Options**, as shown in Figure 9.5.

4 The **Options dialogue box** shown in Figure 9.6 appears.

5 Change the desired options on each tab and then click on **Apply.**

6 To close the **Options dialogue box**, click on **OK.**

There are 11 different tabs in the Options dialogue box that you can use to configure the Windows Media Player to behave in the way you prefer. The tabs include the following options.

■ **Player**—The Player tab (shown in Figure 9.6) gives you several options, including how often you want to check for automatic

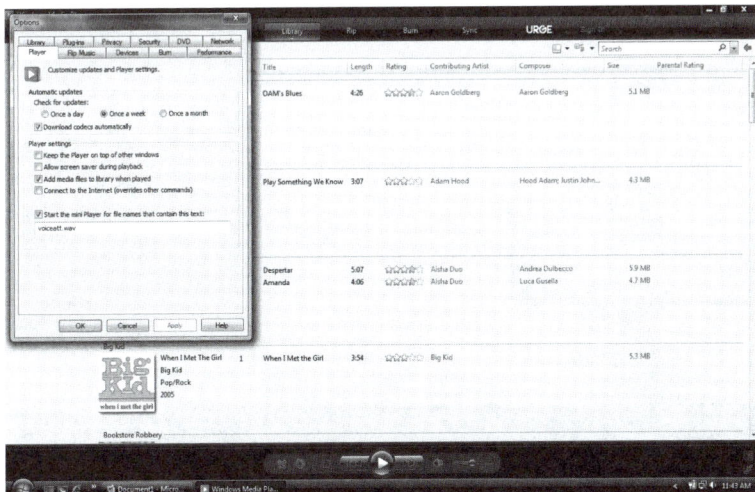

Figure 9.6
The Windows Media Player Options menu.

updates for your Windows Media Player and how you would like to have your player displayed when in use. Select or deselect the desired options.

- **Rip Music**—Changes the location and file format in which music is stored when it is ripped from a CD.

- **Devices**—This tab allows you to make changes to the properties of the devices that your computer uses to play back media files. Select a device and click on **Properties** to choose to change the way that these devices manage your media files.

- **Burn**—On the Burn tab, you can adjust the settings for how music and data files are written to disk, as shown in Figure 9.7.

- **Performance**—The settings on the Performance tab contain options for Internet connection speed, how file buffering is handled and how DVD and video playback is controlled.

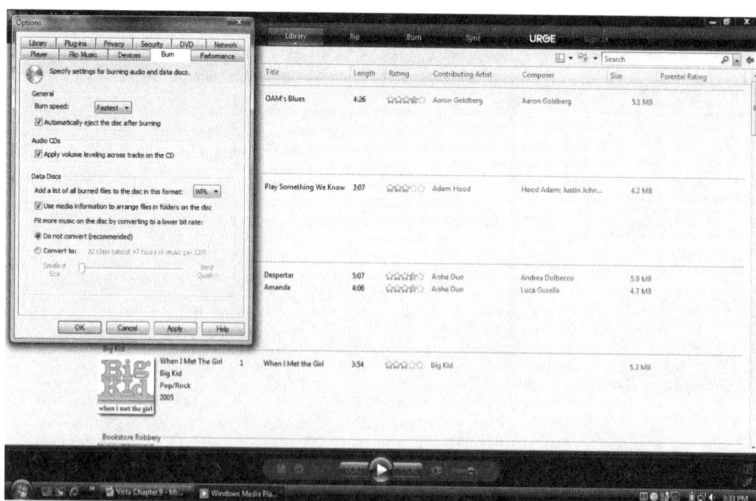

Figure 9.7
Use the Burn tab to determine how files are burned to CDs and DVDs.

Important

The Windows Media Player automatically detects the speed of your Internet connection by default. Unless you have a specific reason for changing the settings on this tab, it's best just to leave them alone.

- **Library**—This tab is where you can change the settings for how your media files are shared and stored in your media library.

- **Plug-ins**—This tab allows you to add and manage plug-ins, as well as remove them. It also allows access to any available property settings for those plug-ins.

- **Privacy**—The Privacy tab (shown in Figure 9.8) allows you to specify Privacy settings. Using these settings, you can customise how cookies are handled, options for media playback and even how your history files are managed.

- **Security**—This tab is to determine which scripts are allowed to run when you are connected to the Internet and what Internet Explorer Zone the Windows Media Player should use.

9

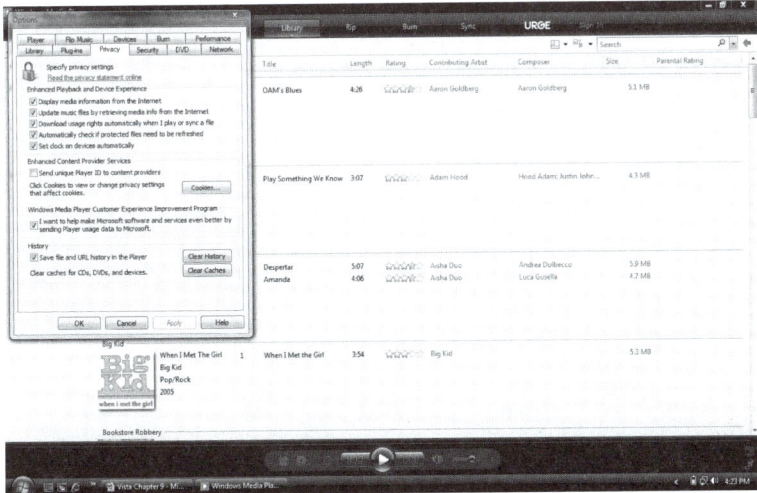

Figure 9.8
The Privacy tab lets you choose privacy options.

Important

Use caution when adjusting security settings. The default Windows security settings are designed to ensure that you are protected from viruses and malware, which could destroy your computer. If you change the settings, you could unknowingly open your computer to attacks by malicious users.

- **DVD**—The DVD tab (shown in Figure 9.9) is where you set rating restrictions and language settings for playing DVDs. Use the rating restrictions to limit the types of DVDs that others play on your computer. Restriction ratings run from no restrictions up to rated 18. Click on the Change button under current rating restrictions to select the level with which you are comfortable.

- **Network**—The Network tab allows you to make adjustments regarding what networks are accessible when using the Windows Media Player.

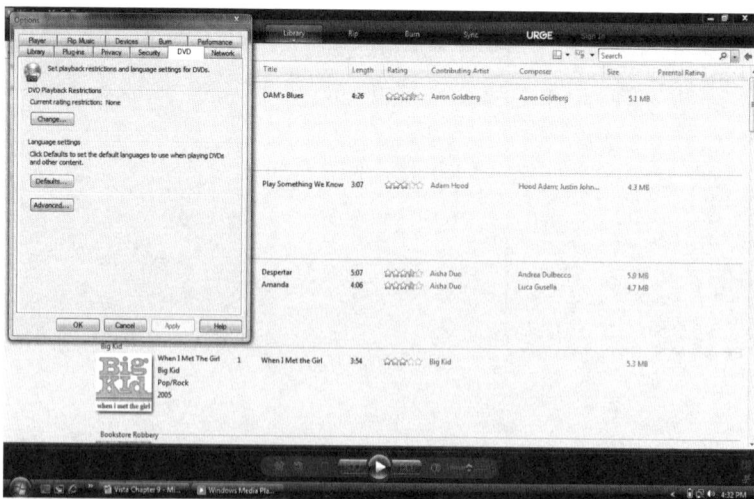

Figure 9.9
The DVD settings tab is used to select rating restrictions and language settings.

> **Important**
>
> Adjusting network settings could cause changes to the way your network behaves. If you change the wrong settings, you could block access to the network completely, so use caution when changing these settings.

Understanding AutoPlay

AutoPlay is the feature that Vista uses to determine how your multimedia and music media will be played when they are inserted into your computer's CD or DVD drive.

9

You can change the settings to suit your personal tastes by following these steps.

1 Go to **Start > Control Panel > Hardware and Sound**.

2 Select **AutoPlay**. The **AutoPlay dialogue box** (shown in Figure 9.10) appears.

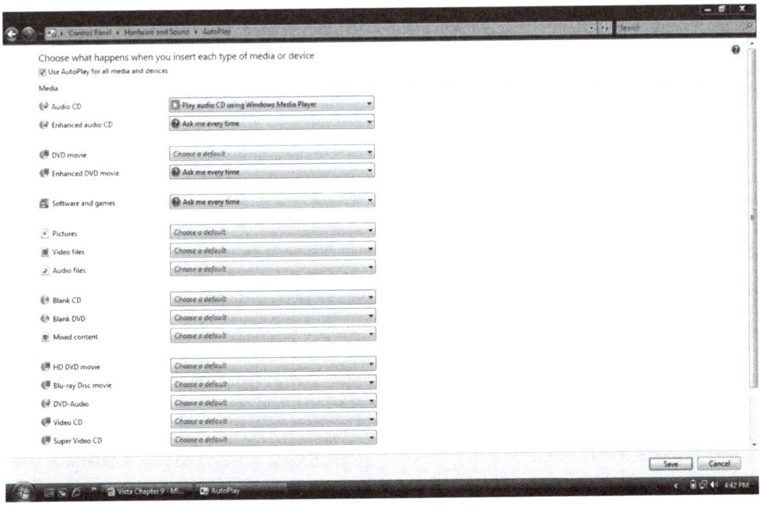

Figure 9.10
The AutoPlay window.

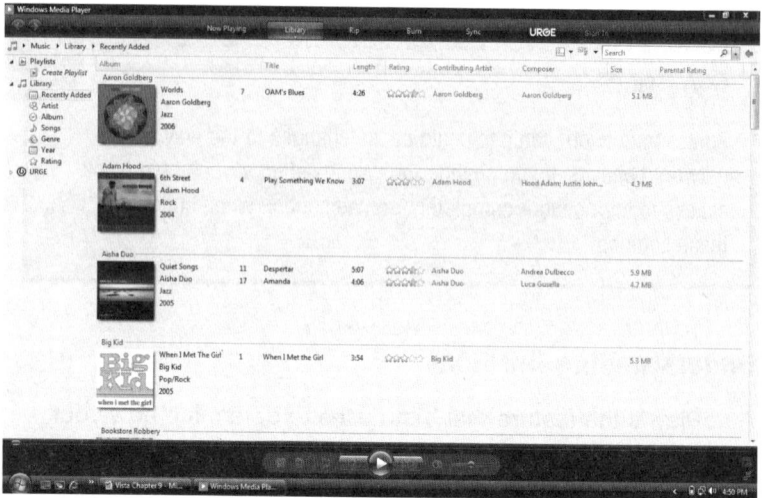

Figure 9.11
The Windows Media Player Library page.

3 For each type of media, select the settings to determine how it is to be handled.

4 When you've finished making your selections, click on **Save** to return to the **control panel**.

5 Then close the **control panel**.

Accessing and Using Your Music Library

Unless you tell your computer to place music and video files in a different folder, they will be saved to the Windows Media Player Library. To access the library, go to **Start > Windows Media Player** and click on the **Library tab**. Your library will be displayed, as shown in Figure 9.11.

The library is divided into categories so that you can search your media in different ways. For example, you can search by album, artist or genre. By clicking on any one of these categories, your media is sorted according to the specifications of that category.

To access the desired file, double-click on it. The file is automatically started in the **Now Playing window** of the Windows Media Player.

To add media files to your library from locations other than the default, follow these steps.

1 Open the **Windows Media Player**.

2 Click on the **Library tab** and select **Add to Library** from the menu that appears.

3 The **Add to Library dialogue box** appears. Select the option that fits the files that you want the Windows Media Player to look for.

4 Click on **Advanced Options** to expand the dialogue box and select specific locations, as shown in Figure 9.12.

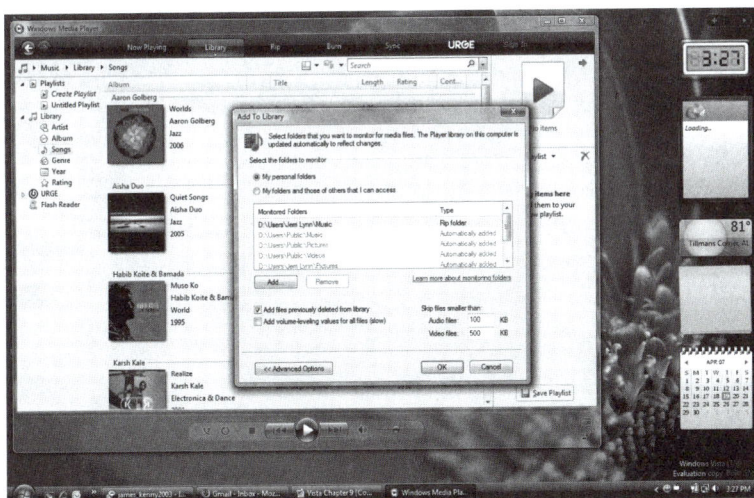

Figure 9.12
Use the Advanced Options button to select specific locations you want the Windows Media Player to monitor.

5 When you've finished making your selections, click on **OK** and the Windows Media Player will search the selected locations for multimedia files.

6 When the search has been completed, click on **Close** and the media library will be updated with any files that were found.

To delete a multimedia file from your library, right-click on that file and select **Delete** from the menu that appears.

Creating a Playlist

You can also access and create playlists from the **Library tab**. To create a playlist, follow these steps.

1 Open the **Windows Media Player**.

2 Click on the **Library tab** to open the **Library menu**.

3 Select **Create Playlist**. The **Playlist task pane** appears on the right side of the Windows Media Player.

4 Type a name for the playlist in the text box provided.

Figure 9.13
Right-click on a title in the playlist to access additional options.

5 Drag the songs from your library to the Playlist task pane to add them to the playlist.

6 To move an item up or down in the playlist, right-click on the title and then select **Move Up** or **Move Down**, as shown in Figure 9.13.

7 When you've finished creating your playlist, select **Save Playlist** to save it on your computer to access in future.

Playing a Playlist

Once you've created a playlist, you'll probably want to listen to it. Playing your playlist is easy. Just double-click on the playlist's name in the Navigation pane on the left side of the Windows Media Player. If you don't see your list there, expand the Playlist file and you should find it.

Ripping and Burning CDs

Jargon buster

Rip means to copy songs from a CD on to your computer. **Burn** means to copy the songs from your playlist on your computer on to a blank CD. You can also burn videos and photos.

The rip feature in the Windows Media Player lets you copy songs from a CD that you have inserted into your CD drive. Once you have a copy of them on your computer, then you can add the songs to a playlist, put them on your MP3 player or copy them on to another disk.

If you are connected to the Internet, the artist information will be listed, but, if not, you can manually add it by right-clicking on the album and songs once the rip has been completed.

To rip a CD, follow these steps.

1 Open the **Windows Media Player**.

2 Insert the disk you want to rip into the CD drive.

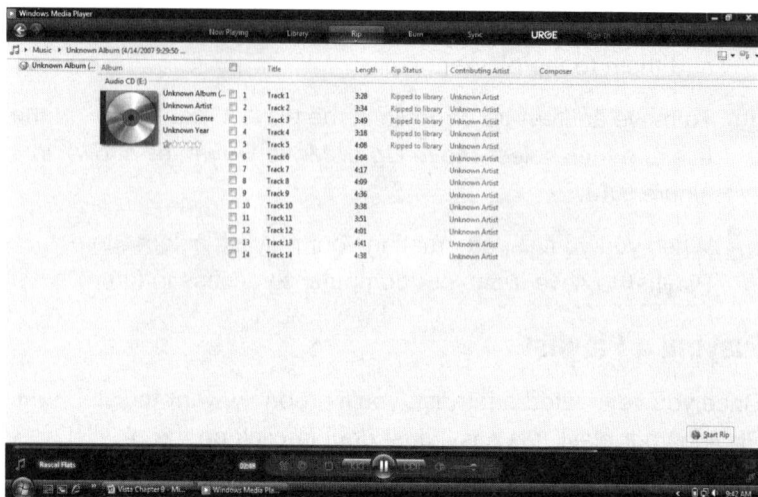

Figure 9.14
Use the Rip menu to select the songs you want to rip from the CD.

3 After the CD has loaded, you should see it listed in the
Windows Media Player. Click on the **Rip tab** at the top of
the Windows Media Player window. This brings up a list of
the songs that are on the CD. Select or deselect the songs
that you would like to rip from the CD, as shown in Figure
9.14.

4 Once the ripping process has begun, if you change your
mind, you can click on the **Stop Rip button** at the bottom
right corner of the window.

5 When the process has finished, the songs that you chose to
copy are then listed in your library.

If you have a CD-RW drive to burn CDs, you can copy your
playlist on to a blank disk. To burn a CD, take the following
steps.

1 Click on the **Burn tab** at the top of the Windows Media
Player window. This will bring up the **Burn menu** (see
Figure 9.15).

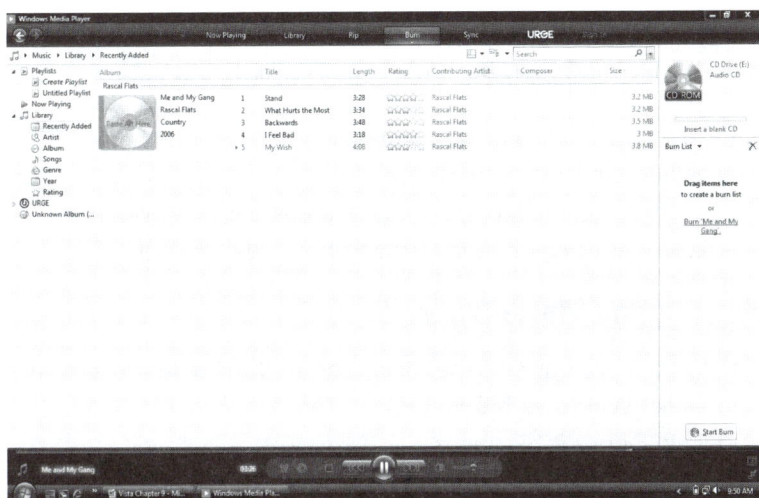

Figure 9.15
Use the Burn menu to select the songs to burn on to a blank CD.

2 Select the songs you want to copy to the CD and drag them to the **Burn List** on the right side of the Windows Media Player window. You can also choose to drag an entire album to the Burn List.

3 Once you have chosen what you would like to copy, insert a writable disk into your CD-RW drive and click on **Start**. The Windows Media Player will begin to copy the selected files to the disk.

4 You are notified when the burn has finished and your CD drive may even open on its own so that you can remove the completed disk.

Important

It is illegal to copy and share copyrighted materials, including movies and music. However, law allows you to create backup copies of any media which you have purchased. The directions that follow are provided strictly for backup purposes, and should not be used for any unlawful copying and sharing of copyrighted materials.

Using Vista's Multimedia Capabilities **135**

→ Using the Windows Movie Maker

With Windows Movie Maker, Vista allows you to edit home videos and pictures, as well as create your own movies. You can import data and media from other sources and use Windows Media Maker to edit it, add to it and take away from it.

Starting the Movie Maker

To start the Windows Movie Maker, go to **Start > All Programs** and select **Windows Movie Maker**. The Windows Movie Maker, shown in Figure 9.16, opens.

Importing Digital Data

You can import digital data to your computer that you would like to use in your videos from digital devices or even from files in your computer to the Movie Maker.

Figure 9.16
The Windows Movie Maker interface.

Importing from a Camera

To transfer images and video to your computer that you have on your camera, plug the camera into your computer (according to the manufacturer's directions) and turn it on. Then follow these steps to upload the images or video on to Windows Movie Maker.

1 In the **Import menu**, on the left side of the screen, select **From digital video camera**, then select **Import**.

2 When prompted, type a name for the file.

3 Select the location to which you would like to save your file.

4 In the **Format** list, select **Windows Media Video (WMV).**

5 You can choose to import the entire list of images or a whole video or just specific images or parts of the video that you want to view. Once you have done this, click on **Next**.

6 Follow the directions on your screen to start importing the data you have chosen.

Importing Existing Media on Your Computer

If you have video or images saved on your computer that you would like to use in the Windows Movie Maker, they too can be imported in to it. Take the following steps to import these videos or images.

1 On the **Import** tab, go to the **Tasks options** and click on **Video.**

2 Select the videos that you would like to import and click on **Import**.

3 For images, choose **Pictures** in the **Tasks options** list instead of Video, then select the pictures that you would like to import and click on **Import**. Your videos or images will be imported into Windows Movie Maker.

You can also import audio files in to the Windows Movie Maker in the same way. Then you'll have audio files to add to movies that you create from still pictures.

Making Movies

Now that you have imported the videos, pictures and audio, it's time to actually use the Windows Movie Maker to make a movie.

To do this, you must put the the clips into some kind of order for them to make sense, then add music and any other background that you would like to have.

If the clips that the Windows Movie Maker has made for you are too big to be manageable, you can split them into smaller chunks by using the **Split command**. To do this, select the clip that you would like to split and then select **Play** from the **Monitor area**.

When the clip reaches the point where you want to split it, press the keyboard combination **Ctrl + M** on your keyboard. This splits the clip in the **Collections area**, leaving the first half of the clip with the original name and the second half with the original name followed by the number 1. You can rename the clips as you wish.

Not only can you split clips in the Windows Movie Maker, you can also put clips together. To combine clips (you can do two or more), take the following steps.

1 Select the clips from the **Collection area** that you would like to combine. Click on the first clip, hold down the **Shift key** and select the rest of the clips that you would like to combine with it.

2 Choose **Clip** and **Combine**. This will combine the clips and save them under the name of the first clip in the selection.

Once you have split and combined the clips as necessary, you should create a storyboard. When you add video and still pictures to your movie, they automatically show up on the storyboard. To put them into the sequence you want, click on and drag them to the **Workspace** in the desired sequence.

Adding Audio

After editing, clipping, combining and sequencing your visual media for your movie, you can add audio to it. You can use background music over existing audio (such as voices), you can use only music or you can even add narration to your movie.

To add audio to your movie, switch to the **Timeline view** and drag and drop music into the **Audio/Music section**. You can then trim the audio clip just as you would a video clip. To adjust the volume of the audio, click on **Tools** and then **Audio** to make the adjustment.

You can even add your voice to the movie as a narrator by clicking on **Tools** and **Narrate Timeline**. Keep in mind that you must have a microphone installed on your computer to do this. Once the **Narrate Timeline menu** is open, choose the type of sound device that you will use to record the narrative. When you are ready to record, click on **Start Narration** and begin speaking your narrative into the microphone. When you have finished, type in a name for the file and save it. It then appears in the **Workspace Timeline** for your movie.

Adding Titles and Credits

There are some simple steps that you can take to add a title to your movie or sections of it and credits at the end. Begin by clicking on **Titles and Credits** in the **Edit category** in the **Task pane**, then take the following steps to create a title for your movie.

1 In the window that appears with the **Titles and Credits pane**, choose the type of title that you would like to add to your movie.

2 Type in the desired name for the title or credit that you would like to add.

3 If you want to change the look of your title or credit, click on **More Options** under the text to make the desired changes.

4 Click on **Add Title**.

Saving and Publishing Movies

To save a movie, choose **File** and **Save Movie File**. Once you have saved a movie file, you can come back to it later to work on it or you can view in the Windows Media Player.

You can also publish your movie, which will allow you to save it to your computer and burn it on to a DVD to hand out to friends and family, record it back to your camera or save it in a smaller format to e-mail to others who would like to view it.

To do this, click on the **Tasks pane** and follow the instructions given. If you wish to burn your movie on to DVD, the Windows DVD Maker will automatically appear when you make that choice.

→ Working with the Windows Slideshow for Digital Pictures

If you have a digital camera that has pictures on it you would like to download on to your computer to save and share, the Windows Slideshow is a great place to do it.

Before using the Windows Slideshow, connect your camera to your computer and follow the onscreen instructions to download your pictures on to your computer.

Viewing and Managing Your Pictures

When you download your pictures on to your computer, you can save them to any folder you like. The default folder is My Pictures, but you can choose to save them in any other folder or create a folder, especially for that group of pictures. Once you have them in a folder, you can manage them in ways that make them easier to access and view. As with any folder in the Vista operating system, you can use the task features on the toolbar to manage your pictures.

By using the View option, you can choose how large your picture icons will be, ranging from small to extra large ones and even a Detailed view, which gives you even smaller icons and pertinent information, or a Tiles view that is similar to the Medium view, but gives you more information about the pictures. Choose the view that will be best for you.

Right-click on a picture to bring up other management features for your pictures, such as editing capabilities. This allows you to change their size, edit out unwanted parts or delete them completely. You can also print your pictures from this menu or set one as your desktop background.

Using the Photo Gallery

The Windows Photo Gallery (see Figure 9.17) is a new feature in the Windows Vista operating system that allows you to put all of your photos in one location and use the available management features from there.

Browse through your pictures and select the one that you would like to view, seeing a full-screen view of it. Then use the toolbar

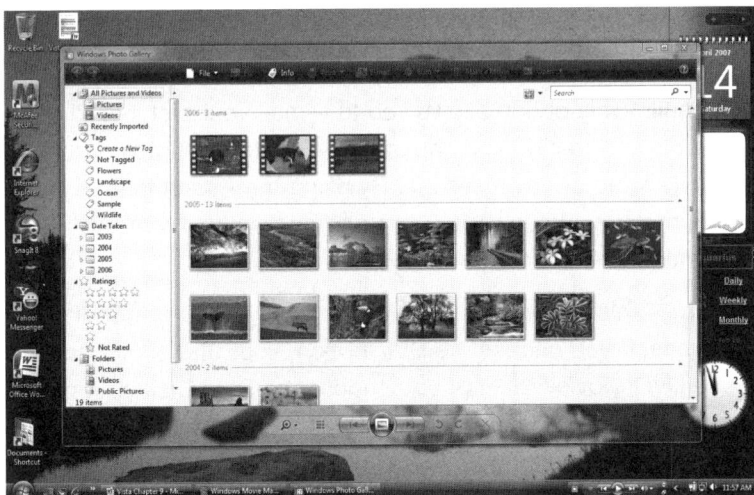

Figure 9.17
The Windows Photo Gallery makes managing your photos easier than before.

options to manage your photos. The toolbar has the following options to help you do this.

- **File**—This dropdown menu enables you to do such tasks as name the photo, delete and duplicate it. You also have an Options feature on this menu that allows you to access the General and Import tabs. These tabs allow you to manage your media and devices in a manner that best suits your needs.

- **Fix**—This option gives you tools that you can use to fix your photos. You can use the Auto Adjust feature to let the computer automatically adjust the colour and exposure of your pictures or you can adjust them yourself using the other menu tools. You can also crop your picture and fix red eye using options in this menu.

- **Info**—This option brings up a menu that lets you view information about your photos. That information includes the date when they were taken and the size of the file.

- **Print**—This option gives you a dropdown menu with two choices – you can either print your pictures or order prints. To order prints, you must have an active Internet connection.

- **E-mail**—This option allows you to e-mail your pictures to friends and family. You can attach a photo or photos or a movie to an e-mail message. By using the Attach feature in this menu, you can resize your photo to make it a more manageable size for e-mailing.

- **Burn**—This option enables you to create a DVD or CD of your photos. If you choose the DVD option, your photos are sent to the DVD Movie Maker. If you choose the Data Disk option, you can burn your photos on to a CD. Use the correct option best suited to the burning drive that you have available.

- **Make a Movie**—This option will allow you to import your photos to the Windows Movie Maker so that you can make a movie with your photos.

- **Open**—This option gives you a list of programs that you can use to open your pictures with. Click on the program that you would like to use to open a specific photo or group of photos.

Printing Your Pictures

As long as you have at least a colour inkjet printer installed on your computer, you can print your pictures. For high-quality pictures, however, it's best to have a photo printer and use the right type of paper. Quality photo paper for printers is readily available.

Windows Vista has a Photo Printing Wizard that walks you through the process of printing your photos. To use the Photo Printing Wizard take the following steps.

1 Double-click on the photo that you want to print.

2 Click on the **Print button** on the toolbar.

3 Use the dropdown menu in the **Print dialogue box** to choose the printer that you would like to print from.

4 Select the size that you would like the printed photo to be.

5 Click on **Print**. Your photos are then printed according to the selections you have made.

Burning Pictures on to a CD

If you have pictures on your camera or computer that you would like to burn on to CD to share with others or so that you have a backup copy and you have a CD-RW drive on your computer, you can use your CD burning program to accomplish this.

To burn a CD, drag the files you would like to include to the CD drive on your computer. When you've finished, click on the **CD Burning balloon** to start the **CD Burning Wizard**.

Using the Windows Slideshow

The Windows Slideshow is a new feature in Vista that allows you to connect a secondary device to your computer (even if it is off) and use it to see information such as your calendar or e-mails. When buying devices to use with this feature, you must make sure that they are compatible with the Vista Windows Slideshow.

Once you have installed the hardware that you are going to use with the Windows Slideshow, access it via the control panel on your computer. You can then determine which features are available for you to use with your device and choose the ones that you would like to have.

10

Securing Windows Vista

In this lesson you'll learn about Windows Security including Firewall and Defender as well as how to configure parental controls.

→ Understanding Windows Security

The most important new features in Vista are probably the least noticeable of them all. They are the new security features that are built into the Vista operating system.

The three major security features in Vista are the Windows Firewall, Windows Defender and the improved parental controls. The Firewall monitors and manages Internet and local network traffic. Windows Defender is a spyware tool that monitors information and data coming to your computer from the Internet, your local network and CDs or DVDs. The parental controls allow you to set up parameters about what websites your children can visit on the Internet, what games they can play and what content they are allowed to view.

The additional security features are designed to help keep you as safe as possible from all of the viruses, worms, malware, Trojans and other security threats that hackers can throw your way.

Using the Windows Firewall

The Windows Firewall is not a new feature to the Windows operating system – it was first included with Windows XP. Although it's been around for a while, it has been improved somewhat for Vista.

Among the improved features in the Windows Firewall is the ability to control it. Accessing it, turning it on and off and managing exceptions is much easier than it was in the past.

> **Important**
>
> Unless you have some other type of firewall installed (and active) on your computer, then you should enable the Windows Firewall. It's especially important that you enable the firewall if you have a home network and have always-on broadband Internet access available on that network. Estimates are that it takes a hacker less than ten minutes to discover an unprotected computer when it is connected to the Internet via broadband.

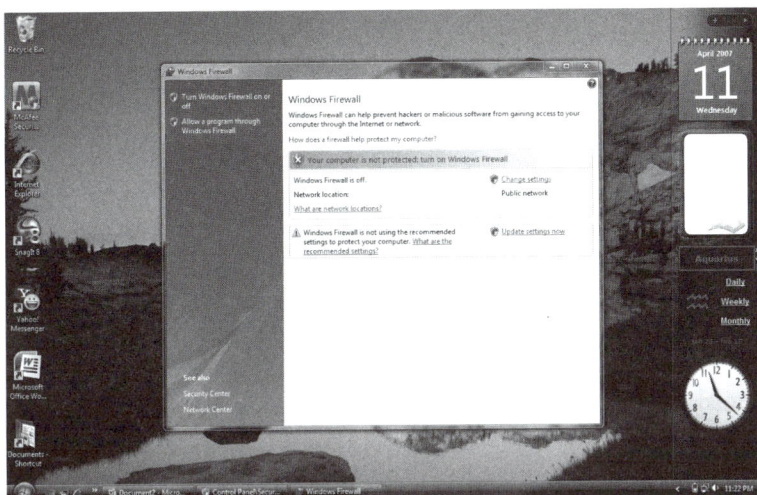

Figure 10.1
The Windows Firewall window.

To access the Windows Firewall, follow these steps.

1 Go to **Start > Control Panel** and click on the **Security icon**.

2 In the screen that appears, click on the **Windows Firewall icon**, to open the **Windows Firewall dialogue box** (shown in Figure 10.1).

3 From this dialogue box, you can start, configure and turn off your Windows Firewall.

Starting and Configuring the Windows Firewall

Once the Windows Firewall dialogue box is open, you can quickly tell whether or not your Firewall is on. In the white portion of the dialogue box, you'll see a section that is either green or red. If it is green, that means your Firewall is on and is set as recommended. If the section is red, then either your Firewall is turned off or it is not set using the recommended settings.

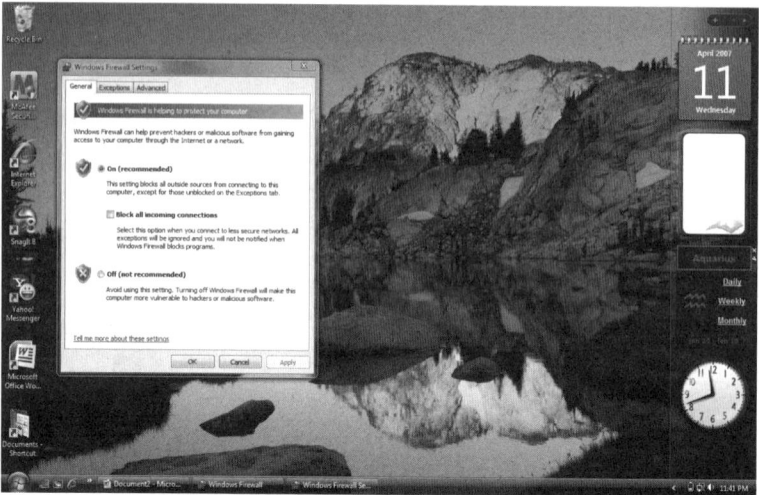

Figure 10.2
The Windows Firewall Settings dialogue box for turning the Firewall on or off.

If your Windows Firewall is turned off, you can start it by clicking on the link at the top left of the dialogue box that reads "Turn Windows Firewall on or off". This opens the **Windows Firewall Settings dialogue box** (shown in Figure 10.2). Click on the button next to **On (recommended)**. Your Windows Firewall is now active.

Timesaver tip

Windows Vista features a security capability called the **user account control (UAC)**. This control is set to prompt users for permission before they make changes to the operating system features. The UAC has been known to create some issues with activities such as installing printers, networking and managing hardware devices. If you find that you are experiencing difficulties and can't figure out why, try turning the UAC off.

To do that, go to **Start > Control Panel > User Accounts and Family Safety > User Accounts**. Then select **Turn User Account Control on or off.** In the dialogue box that appears, deselect the user account control options and click on **OK**. You can always turn this option back on later.

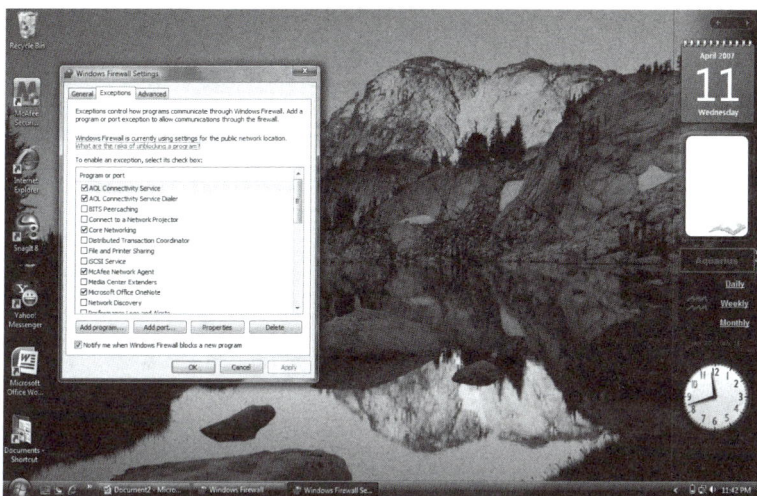

Figure 10.3
The Windows Firewall Settings Exceptions tab.

To configure which programs are allowed through your Windows Firewall, select the Exceptions tab in the Windows Firewall Settings dialogue box (as shown in Figure 10.3).

To enable or disable one of the programs on the list, select or deselect the box next to the program name. Using the default settings here is best, but, if you know that a site is trustworthy, put a tick in the box next to its name by clicking on it and then click on **Apply** and then **OK** to save the setting changes.

The Advanced tab (see Figure 10.4) allows you to select the connections that you would like the Windows Firewall to protect. By default, all of the connections available on your computer are protected. Unless you are using a different firewall, it is recommended that you leave the default settings as they are.

Stopping the Windows Firewall

Sometimes when you install programs, you are directed to turn your firewall off before the installation process begins.

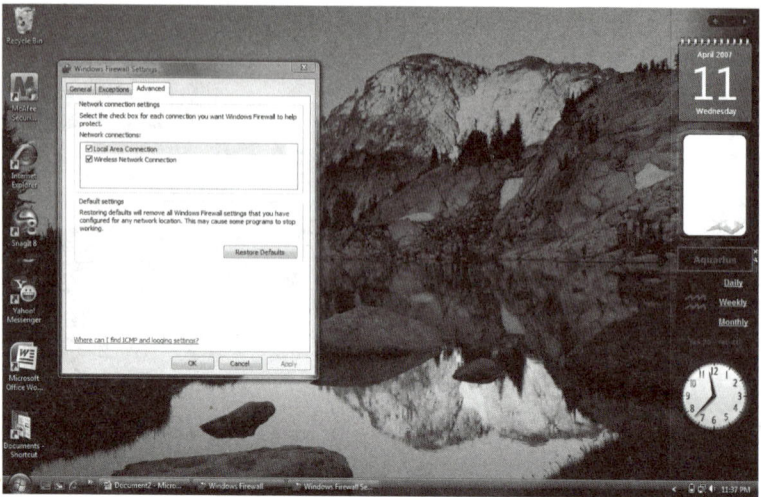

Figure 10.4
The Windows Firewall Settings Advanced tab.

To turn the Windows Firewall off, follow these steps.

1 Go to the **Control Panel** and select **Security**. When the Security window opens, click on the **Turn Windows Firewall on or off link** under the Windows Firewall icon.

2 In the **Windows Firewall Settings dialogue box** that appears, click on the button next to **Off**.

3 Click on **Apply** and then on **OK** to save your setting.

→ Using Windows Defender

Windows Defender is a tool that can identify and remove spyware from your computer. Spyware is a type of program that can install on your computer without you knowing it and gather information about you and your computer. Because spyware typically requires a lot of resources to report collected information, it can make your computer perform much more slowly than it should.

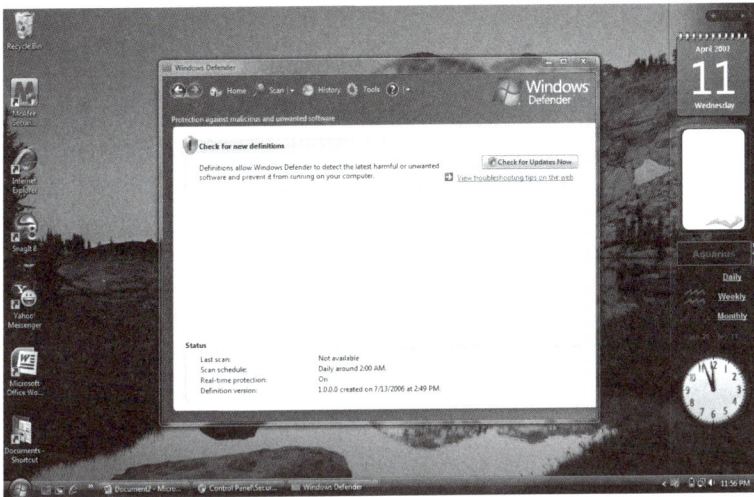

Figure 10.5
The Windows Defender dialogue box.

Windows Defender runs in real time and is constantly monitoring programs that are installed on your computer. To access it go to **Start > Control Panel**, click on **Security** and then select the **Windows Defender icon**. This opens the **Windows Defender dialogue box** (shown in Figure 10.5).

Using Windows Defender Tools

To configure Windows Defender, select the **Tools icon** from the available icons at the top of the dialogue box. This takes you to the **Tools and Settings page** of the dialogue box, as can be seen in Figure 10.6.

In the **Settings section** of the page, you'll find the **Options link**. Click on it to be taken to a page where you can customise how Windows Defender runs on your computer. After you've made your selections, click on **Save** and you're returned to the **Windows Defender dialogue box**. There you also have an option to join **Microsoft SpyNet** – a community of users who allow information from Windows Defender to be collected and shared.

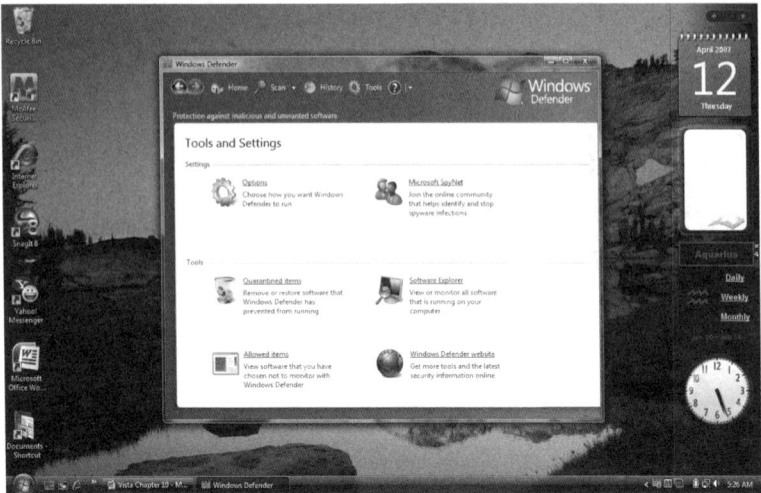

Figure 10.6
The Windows Defender Tools and Settings page.

Also in the dialogue box are several tools to help you maximise
the security of your computer. You'll find these in the **Tools
section** of the dialogue box and they include the following.

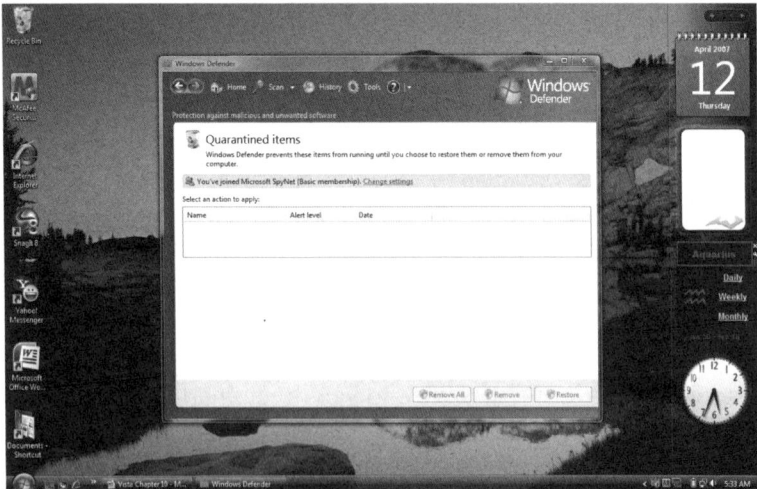

Figure 10.7
The Windows Defender Quarantined items page.

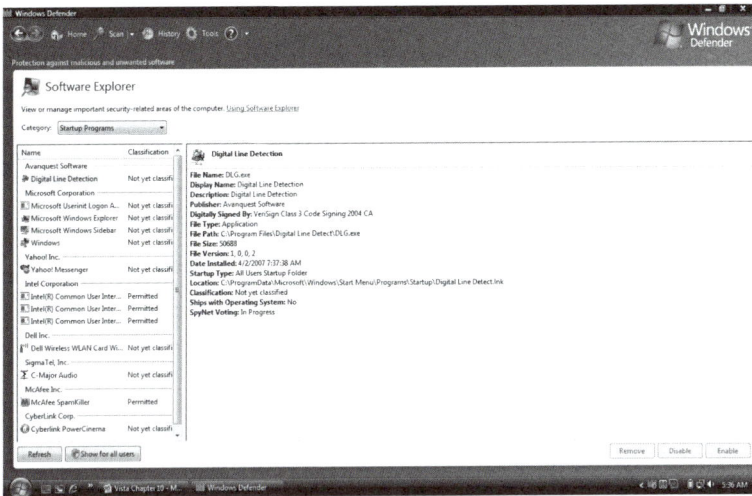

Figure 10.8
The Windows Defender Software Explorer page.

- **Quarantined items**—When Windows Defender stops a program because it suspects it to be spyware, that program is placed in a holding area, or quarantine. By clicking on the Quarantined items icon, you access a page listing all such programs and then you can choose to delete the program completely or restore it (see Figure 10.7).

- **Software Explorer**—The Software Explorer (shown in Figure 10.8), allows you to view and monitor all software that is running on your computer. You can scroll through the list at the left of the window to select a program. The details about that program are then shown in the information pane on the right. You have the option to remove or disable each software program that is running at the time.

- **Allowed items**—The Allowed items page (see Figure 10.9), shows you what programs you have allowed Windows Defender to install on your computer.

- **Windows Defender website**—The Windows Defender website link allows you to connect to the Internet, go to the

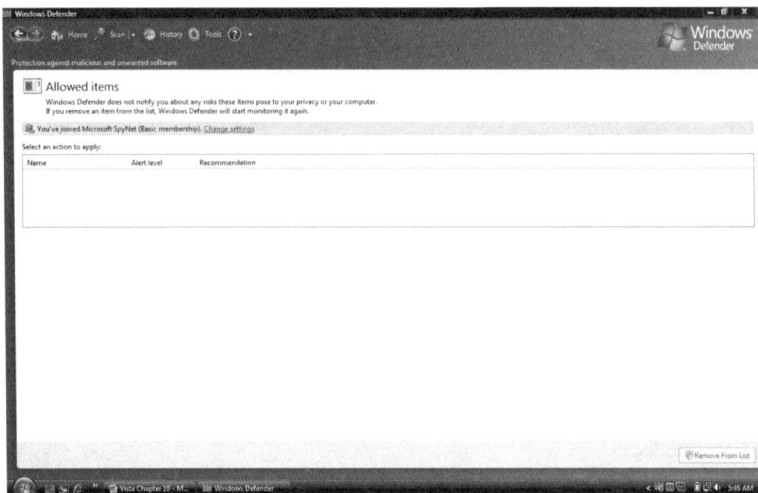

Figure 10.9
The Windows Defender Allowed items page.

website and get the latest tools and security information for Windows Defender.

Running a Windows Defender Scan

You can run a Windows Defender scan on your computer by clicking on **Scan** in the Windows Defender **Tools and Settings window**. This will begin a Quick Scan on your computer (see Figure 10.10). The quick scan only scans the most used areas of your hard drive. When it has finished, you will see information about the time the scan started, how long it took and how many files it scanned. If you prefer to run a more inclusive scan, you can select the dropdown menu to choose a full scan, or a custom scan.

When you open the Scan window, it asks if you would like to check for updates. In order to update Windows Defender, you must have an active Internet connection.

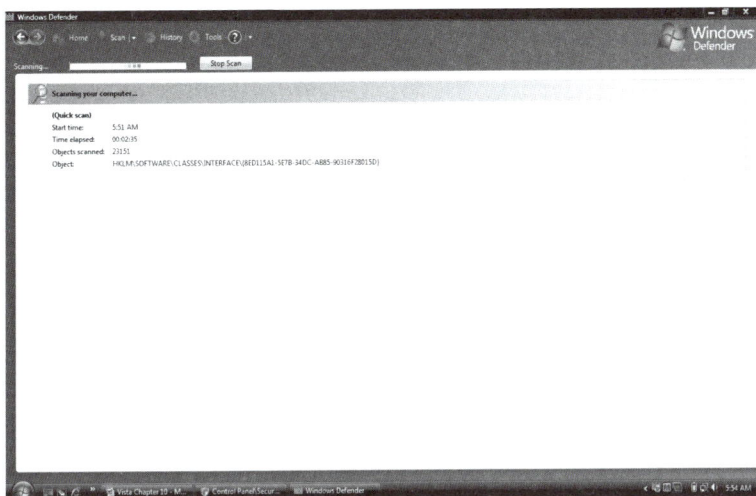

Figure 10.10
A Windows Defender quick scan in progress.

→ Configuring Parental Controls

The Vista operating system also has parental control settings, which have been vastly improved compared with previous versions of the operating system.

Parental controls allow you to choose the online content your child sees while using the computer, as well as what areas of the computer the child is allowed to access, what games he or she can play and even how long he or she can use the computer.

Important

To set the parental controls, each child needs a user account. Make sure that your administrator account is password protected before creating these accounts so that your child cannot access your account and change the settings you have selected.

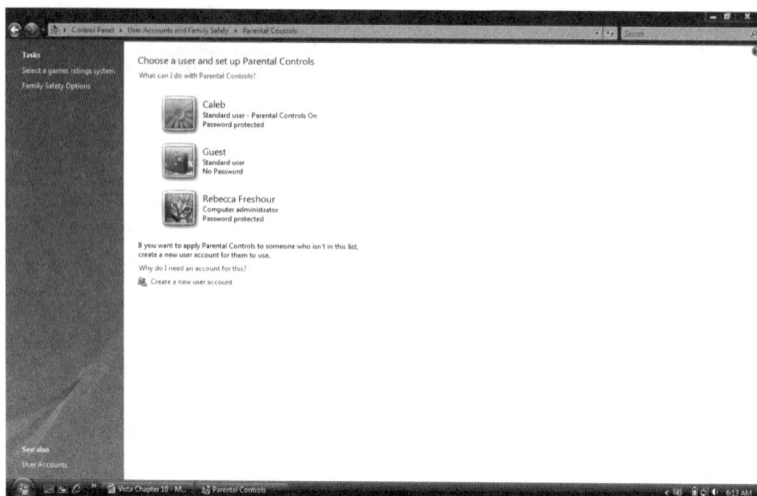

Figure 10.11
Choose the user account that you would like to apply parental controls to.

To configure the parental controls, take the following steps.

1 Go to **Start > Control Panel** and select **User Accounts and Family Safety**.

2 In the **Security dialogue box** that opens, select **Parental Controls**.

3 When the **Parental Controls window** opens, select the user account you would like to set the parental controls for, as shown in Figure 10.11.

4 In the **User Controls dialogue box** that opens, click on the button next to **On** to enable the parental controls.

5 Next, click on the button next to **On** for Activity Reporting, as shown in Figure 10.12. This allows you to receive reports showing how your child is using the computer.

6 Now you can set what restrictions you would like to apply to this account. Click on the link for **Windows Vista Web Filter.** As shown in Figure 10.13, the **Web Restrictions dialogue box** opens.

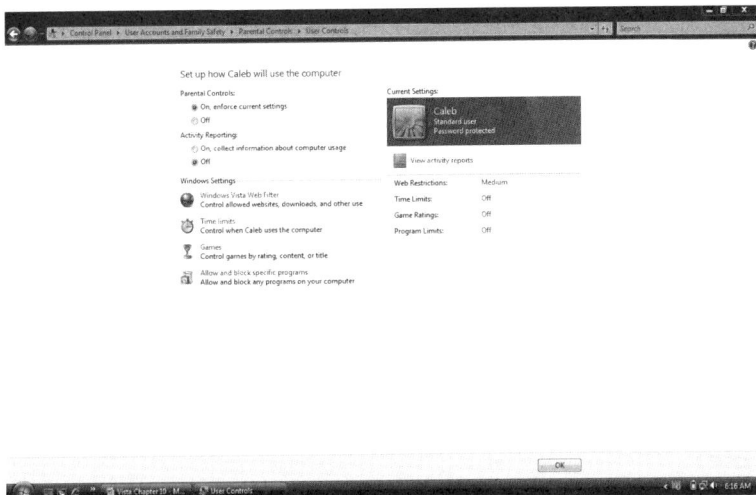

Figure 10.12
The User Controls dialogue box.

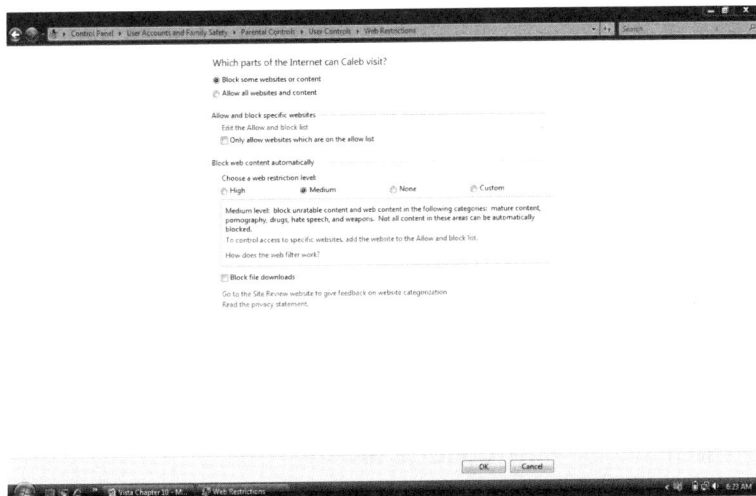

Figure 10.13
The Web Restrictions dialogue box.

7 Select the web restrictions that you would like to apply to your child's user account. You can choose to **block** or **allow** websites, set the restriction level and block file downloads.

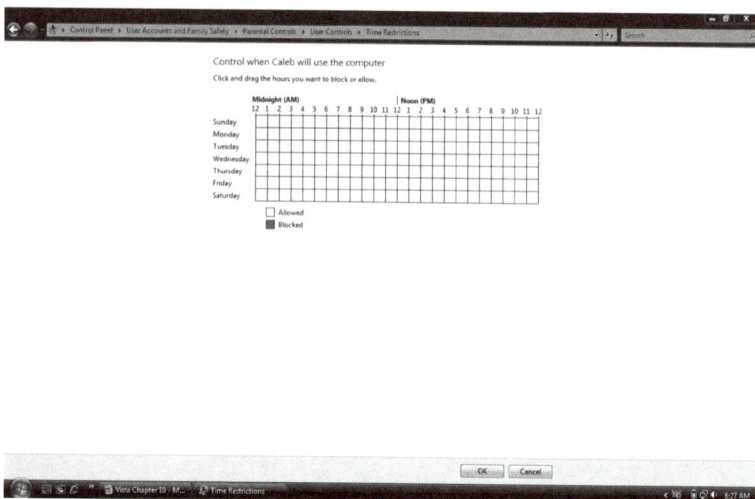

Figure 10.14
The Time Restrictions dialogue box.

8 After you have set the web restrictions, click on **OK** to save your settings and return to the **User Controls dialogue box**.

9 Next, select **Time Restrictions** in the **User Controls window** to limit the amount of time you will allow your child to be on the computer. The **Time Restrictions dialogue box** (shown in Figure 10.14) appears.

10 To set the time limits, click and drag the boxes with the times you do not wish your child to use the computer. When you have finished, click on **OK** to save your settings and return to the **User Controls dialogue box**.

11 To control which games your child plays on the computer, select the **Games link** in the **User controls dialogue box**. This opens the **Game Controls dialogue box** (shown in Figure 10.15), which allows you to set restrictions on the types of games your child can access.

12 Choose what games your child is allowed to play in terms of their ratings by clicking on the **Set game ratings link**.

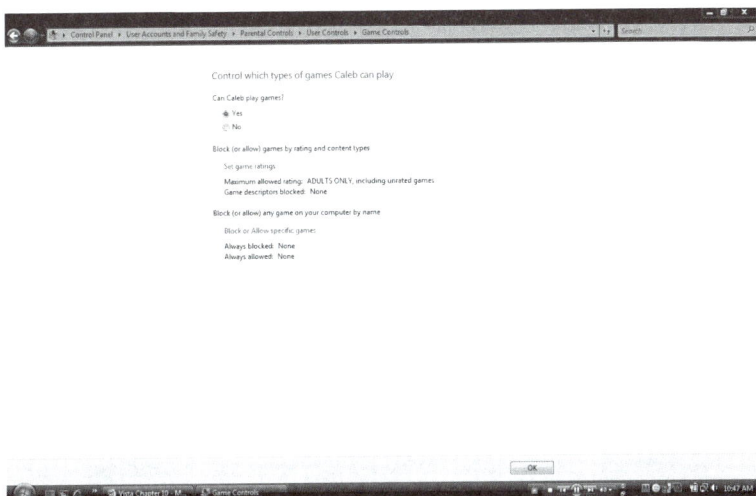

Figure 10.15
The Game Controls dialogue box.

10

Alternatively, you can block or allow specific games by choosing the **Block or Allow specific games link**.

13 After you have made your selections, click on **OK** to return to the **User Controls dialogue box**.

14 The last option available is the **Allow and block specific programs link**, which takes you to to the **Application Restrictions dialogue box** shown in Figure 10.16 overleaf. Here you can choose from the options for your child to use all programs or only certain programs. Click on the button you choose.

15 If you choose to block programs, a list of the programs available on the computer appears in the dialogue box shown in Figure 10.17 overleaf. Click on the boxes beside the programs that you would like to allow your child to view, which will place a tick in them, and deselect any inappropriate options.

16 When you've finished making your selections, click on **OK** to save your settings and return to the **User Controls dialogue**

Securing Windows Vista **159**

box. Click on **OK** again to return to the **Parental Controls dialogue box** and then close that box.

> ## Important
>
> Remember to repeat this process for each of the accounts you need to set up parental controls for. Because you have to repeat the process for each account, you can set different levels of parental controls for each of your children.

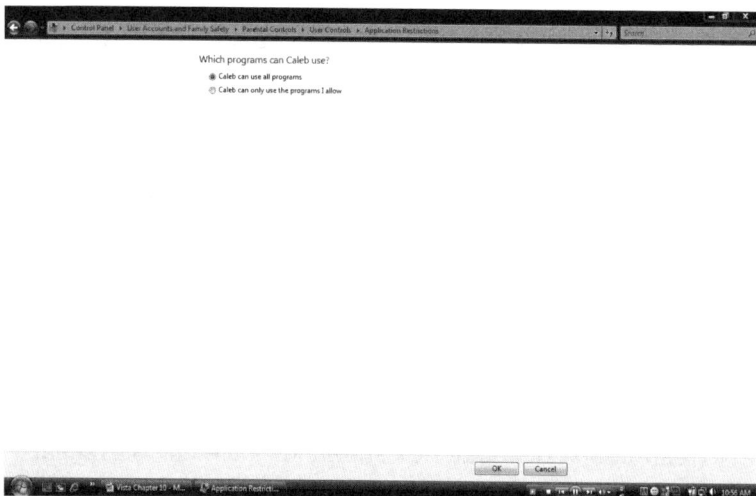

Figure 10.16
The Appliction Restriction options.

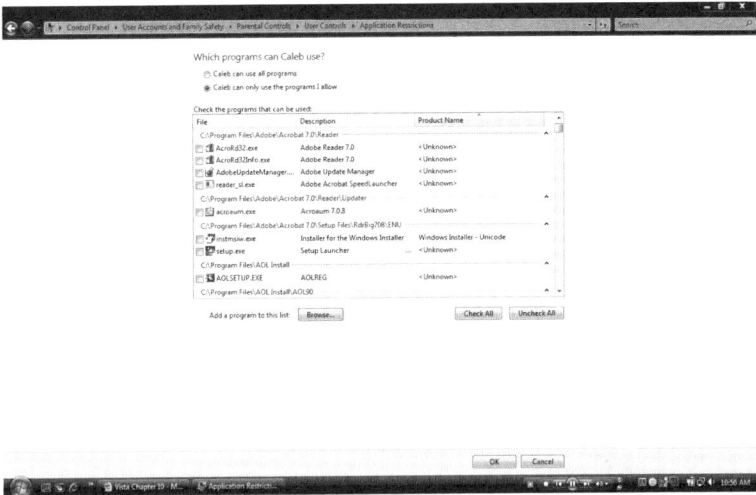

Figure 10.17
Select the programs you want to block.

11

Using Remote Desktop Access

In this lesson you'll learn how to enable, configure and connect using Remote Access. You'll also learn about Remote Assistance.

→ Understanding Remote Access

Remote Access allows you to access another Windows computer from the computer that you are using via an Internet connection. For example, if you are at work and want to access your computer at home, you can do so by means of Remote Access. You can also access a Windows computer that someone else is on to help troubleshoot problems that he or she is having with programs or applications.

Enabling Remote Access

Important

You must be logged on to your computer as the administrator to enable the Remote Access option and allow others to connect to it. If you do not have administrator privileges, ask the person who does to enable this option for you.

To enable Remote Access, follow these steps.

1 Go to **Start > Control Panel > System and Maintenance**.

2 Select the **Remote Access link** below the **System option**. This opens the **System Properties dialogue box** to the **Remote tab**, as shown in Figure 11.1.

3 To allow Remote Access, select **Allow Remote Assistance connections to this computer**.

4 Click on the **Advanced button** to set a time limit on others accessing your computer.

5 The **Remote Assistance Settings dialogue box** appears. Set a time limit and click on **OK** to return to the **System Properties dialogue box**.

6 If you want to be able to connect to the computer you are using from another, then also select one of the allow options in the **Remote Desktop** section of the dialogue box.

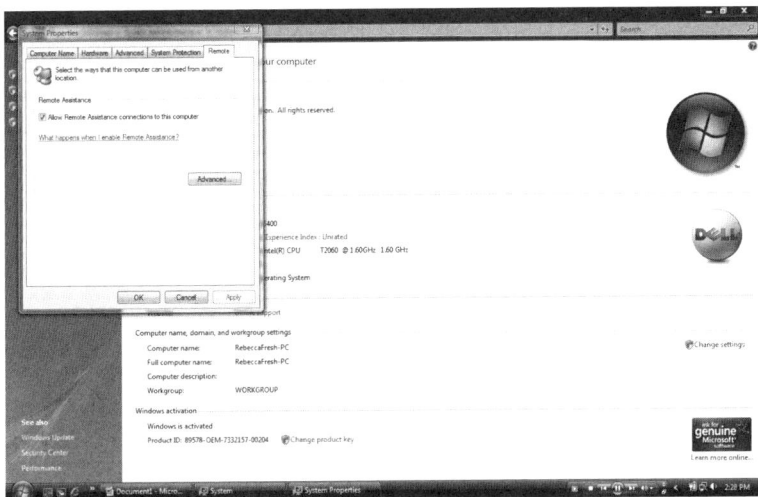

Figure 11.1
Use the System Properties dialogue box to set Remote Access options.

7 Next, click on the **Select Users button** to narrow down the number of people who have access to your computer.

8 Highlight the users you will allow in the **Remote Desktop Users dialogue box** that appears. Then click on **OK** to save your settings and return to the **System Properties dialogue box**.

9 In the **System Properties dialogue box**, click on **Apply** and then **OK** to save your settings and close the **System Properties dialogue box**. Remote Access is now enabled.

Configuring Remote Access

If the computer that you are enabling Remote Access on is running in Windows Vista or XP when you enable Remote Desktop on the host computer, you will not have to do anything to configure Remote Access because it will already be automatically configured for you.

If the computer you're using is not a Vista or XP computer, however, then you will have to install the Remote Desktop

Connection software. This software can be found on the Windows Vista installation CD or can be downloaded from: www.microsoft.com/windowsxp/downloads/tools/rdclientdl.mspx

The software works for almost any version of Windows. Follow the onscreen instructions that appear when the installation process is started.

Connecting Using Remote Access

Once the host and remote computers have been configured, you can connect from one computer to another using Remote Access. To do this on the remote computer, take the following steps.

1 Go to **Start > All Programs > Accessories** and select **Remote Desktop Connection**.

2 In the **Remote Desktop Computer dialogue box** that appears, enter the name or TCP/IP address of the computer you are connecting to or select it from the dropdown menu, then click on **Connect**.

3 The computer will go through a visual connection process. Once you are connected, enter your user name and password and click on **OK**. You now have access to the host computer.

Managing Remote Access

If you use a dial-up connection to connect to a remote computer, you may need to change and tweak some of the settings for the connection and other areas of use.

Timesaver tip

It is not recommended that you use the Remote Access feature via dial-up if you can avoid it. Dial-up Internet access is much slower than broadband and you'll find that the Remote Access program is jerky and slow. It may even hang up on you or boot you out of the connection completely. If at all possible, use Remote Access with broadband.

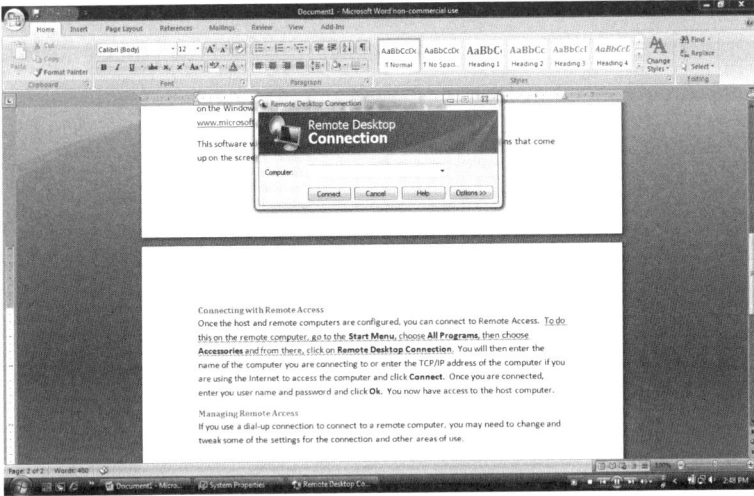

Figure 11.2
The Remote Desktop Connection dialogue box.

11

To manage your Remote Access connection, follow these steps.

1 Go to **Start > All Programs > Accessories > Remote Desktop Connection**. The Remote Desktop Connection dialogue box (shown in Figure 11.2) opens.

2 Click on the **Options button** to expand the **Remote Desktop Connection menu** so it is as shown in Figure 11.3.

3 In the **Remote Desktop Connection dialogue box**, there are several tabs to help you manage your Remote Access. The **Experience tab** lets you choose your connection speed and which features you would like to allow once you have opened a window on the host computer. You can also automatically reconnect if the connection is lost by selecting the option at the bottom of that dialogue box.

4 The **Display tab** enables you to choose how you want your display to look once you have connected to the host computer. You can choose to view it in full screen and decide on the quality of the colours that are seen while connected. At the bottom of the menu, select the box to

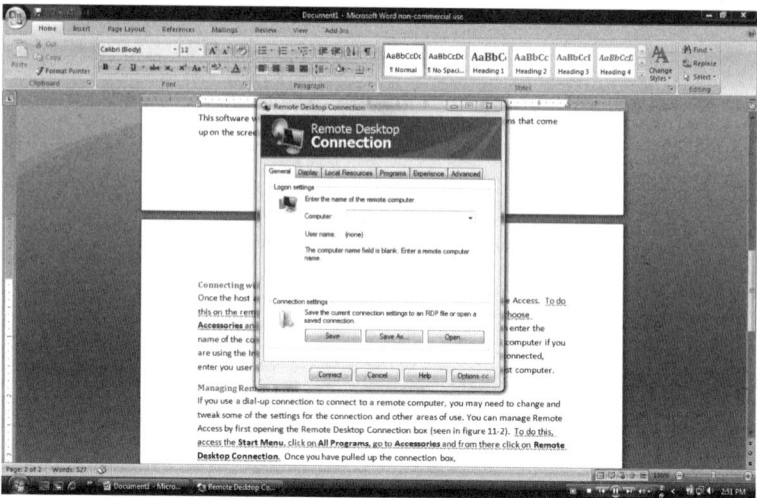

Figure 11.3
Remote Desktop Connection menu.

display the connection bar while in full-screen mode if you would like to keep it visible at all times.

5 There are also **General, Local Resources, Programs** and **Advanced tabs** available. Use these tabs to customise your Remote Access experience.

6 When you have finished configuring your settings, click on **Connect** to connect to another computer using **Remote Access.**

→ Using the Remote Assistance

Remote Assistance was first introduced with Windows XP and allows a more experienced user, or Expert, to view the desktop of another, less experienced user, or Novice, when authorised by the Novice to do so. Both users must be connected to Remote Assistance simultaneously, on the same network and be using Windows Vista or XP. The user of the Novice computer must have administrative capabilities to allow the Expert to access the computer using Remote Assistance.

Activating Remote Assistance

Follow these steps to activate Remote Assistance:

1 Go to **Start > Control Panel** and select **System Properties**.

2 In **System Properties**, select the **Remote Settings** link, to the left of the window.

3 Place a tick in the box next to **Allow Remote Assistance Invitations to Be Sent from This Computer** by clicking on it.

4 Once Remote Assistance has been enabled, select the **Advanced button** to use the **Settings box** to allow remote control of your computer to take place. If you do not tick this box, the remote user will be able to see your computer, but not be able to use it. You can specify how long you would like for the remote user to be allowed to remain on or return to your computer in this window also.

5 When you have finished choosing these settings, click on **OK** to save them and close the dialogue box.

Accessing Remote Assistance

Once a user has enabled Remote Assistance, he or she can access it for help with troubleshooting issues for the computer. The best place to start when issues arise is **Help and Support**. To access **Help and Support**, go to **Start** and select **Help and Support**.

When the **Help and Support menu** appears, there is a section entitled **Use Remote Assistance**. Select this option to **Invite someone you trust to help you**, which brings up a window that will allow you to invite someone on to your computer using Remote Assistance. To use the Remote Assistance options, you must have an active Internet connection in order to enable the remote user to help you.

Once you have chosen to allow someone to help you, you can then choose how to invite them — either via e-mail or by using a disk.

Once you have chosen which option you want to use, follow the onscreen instructions to complete and send the invitation. Once the invitation has been sent and received, the chosen user can then access your computer and start helping you troubleshoot your chosen issues.

12

Using System Tools

In this lesson you'll learn about using System Information, Windows Update and System Restore as well as how to defragment the hard drive.

→ Scheduling Maintenance Tasks

System tools allow you to perform routine maintenance on your computer to keep it operating at maximum efficiency. However, these tools can temporarily slow your computer down or even make it unusable while the maintenance is being performed, so you can schedule tasks such as updates or Disk Cleanup for times when your computer won't be in use.

To use the Task Scheduler to create a maintenance schedule for Disk Cleanup, follow these steps.

1 Go to **Start > Control Panel**, and select **System and Maintenance**.

2 In the **System Maintenance dialogue box**, look for **Administrative Tools**. Under it, click the **Schedule Tasks link**. This opens the **Task Scheduler dialogue box** shown in Figure 12.1.

3 In the **Task Scheduler dialogue box**, click on **Action**.

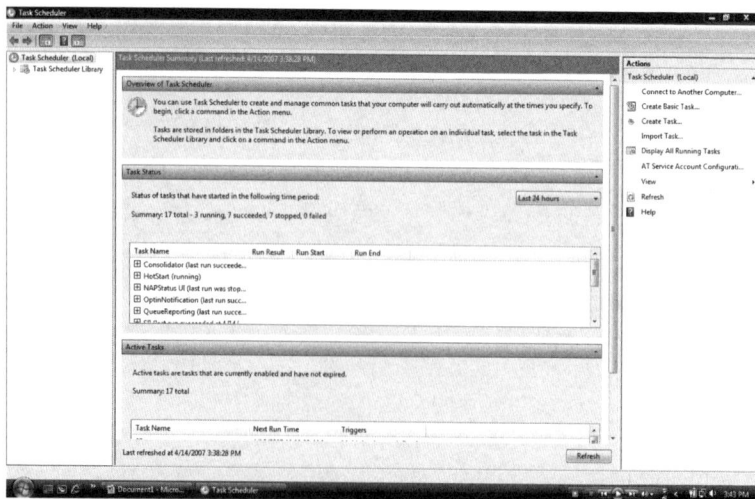

Figure 12.1
Use the Task Scheduler to set up your computer to do useful tasks that save time.

4 Then select **Create Basic Task**. The **Create Basic Task Wizard** opens.

5 In the text boxes provided, type a name for the task you are creating and then type a description of that task. When you've finished, click on **Next**.

6 On the next screen you need to select a trigger for your task. Select the trigger, then click on **Next**.

7 Depending on the time frame you have selected, the next screen may prompt you to provide details about that time frame. For example, when you choose to perform a task monthly, you're prompted to select the months, the day of the month and even the start time for the task. When you have made these selections, click on **Next**.

8 The next screen is the **Action screen**. On this screen, select the action that you would like to happen when the trigger is reached. In this case, select **Start a program** and then click on **Next**.

9 The next screen is where things get a little difficult. Here you need to tell the Scheduler which program to start. As you're scheduling the Disk Cleanup to run at regular intervals, click on the **Browse button**.

10 In the **Open dialogue box**, navigate to and select **cleanmgr**, then click on **Open**. You're returned to the **Task Scheduler Wizard**.

11 Click on **Next** to review the settings for the task you are scheduling. If you're happy with those settings, click on **Finish**. Your task is now set to run as you've specified.

You can also create task schedules for other actions, such as updates for Vista. All you need to do is set a schedule for each of the routine maintenance tasks that you would like performed.

12

→ Using System Information

You can use the System page (shown in Figure 12.2), to view basic information about your computer, such as your hardware configuration, the software environment you're operating in, and even what type of computer resources you have available to you. This information comes in handy if you are trying to troubleshoot issues or find out if you have enough resources to operate hardware or software programs.

To open the System page, start from the **Control Panel** and click on **System and Maintenance**. From the **System and Maintenance menu**, choose **System**. You can now view the information on that page.

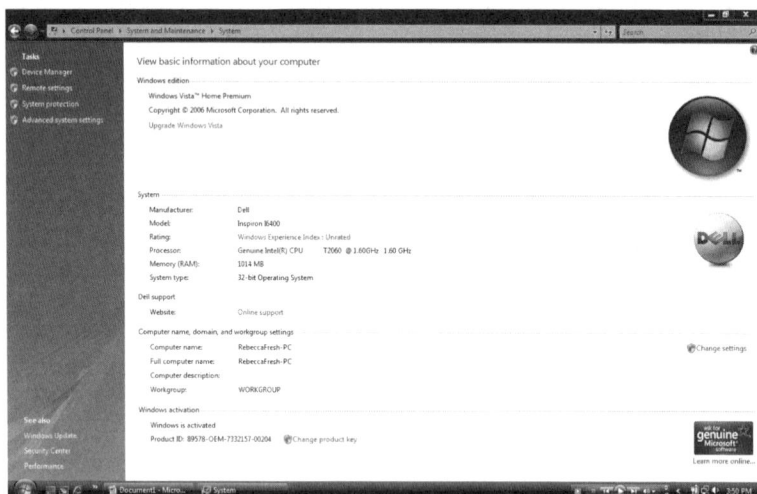

Figure 12.2
Use the System page to learn about your computer's resources.

→ Using Windows Update

The Windows Update feature allows you to apply updates to Vista automatically as they become available from Microsoft. Windows Update is turned on automatically as a default setting, but you can access the Windows Update menu to customise the options and change the settings.

To change your update settings, do the following.

1 Go to **Control Panel > System and Maintenance** and select **Windows Update**. This brings up the **Windows Update dialogue box** (shown in Figure 12.3).

2 Select **Change Settings** from the menu on the left. This opens the **Change settings dialogue box** (shown in Figure 12.4). There are several options to choose from. Here is a brief overview of each one.

- **Install updates automatically**—This setting is selected by default. Windows checks for updates automatically,

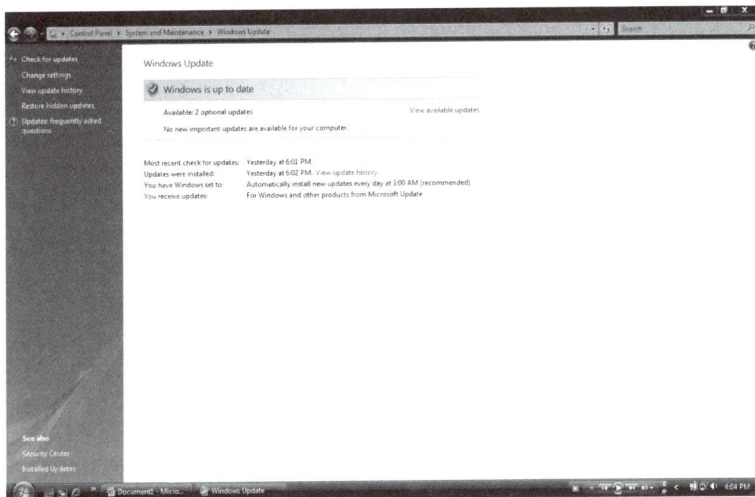

Figure 12.3
Use the Windows Update dialogue box to customise your update settings.

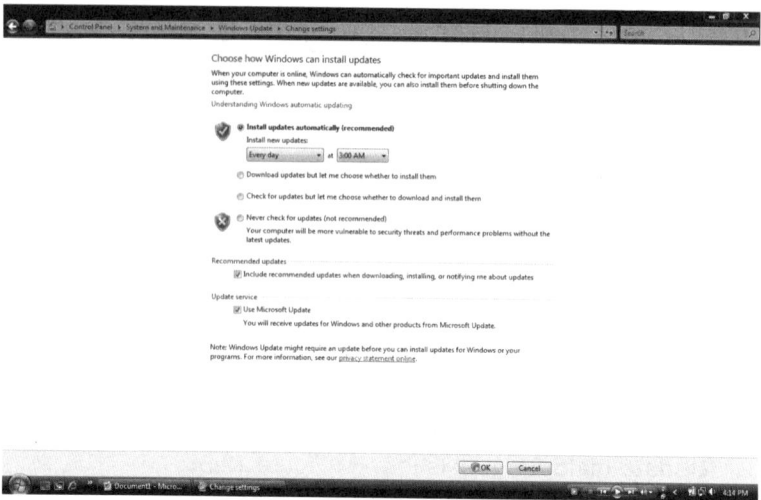

Figure 12.4
Use the Change settings dialogue box to choose how updates are installed on your computer.

downloads them and installs them on your computer without any interaction with you. Notice that you have the option of choosing when Windows will install your updates. Keep in mind that you must be connected to the Internet to install the updates, so choose a time when Internet Explorer will be open.

■ **Download updates but let me choose whether to install them**—If you choose this option, Windows will download the updates for you, but, rather than installing them automatically, it will prompt you with a message telling you that you have updates that are ready to install. You can then select which of those updates you would like to have installed.

■ **Check for updates, but let me choose whether to download and install them**—Selecting this option allows Windows to check for updates, but it will not download or install them without your permission to do so. Windows prompts you with a message when updates have been found.

- **Never check for updates**—By choosing this option, Windows will never check for updates automatically. When you want to find updates, you will have to do it yourself. *This option is not recommended by Microsoft.*

3 Change the settings to reflect your personal preferences, then click on **OK** to save them.

> ### Important
>
> It is recommended that you change your automatic update settings only if you are familiar with the consequences of those changes. Not properly updating your computer can leave it vulnerable to attacks by malicious hackers or leave program and application errors unfixed. Use caution when changing your update settings.

→ Using System Restore

12

Have you ever made changes to your computer and then wished you could undo them? Vista's System Restore option allows you to do just that, returning your computer to how it was set up at some point in the past when it was working properly.

Creating a Restore Point

System Restore works by creating restore points, which are points in your computer's history when it has been working properly.

> ### Important
>
> System Restore will only restore your operating system and applications to their previous state. It will not restore files that have been lost or deleted. For that reason, it's always best to keep a backup copy of all files and documents that are stored on your computer.

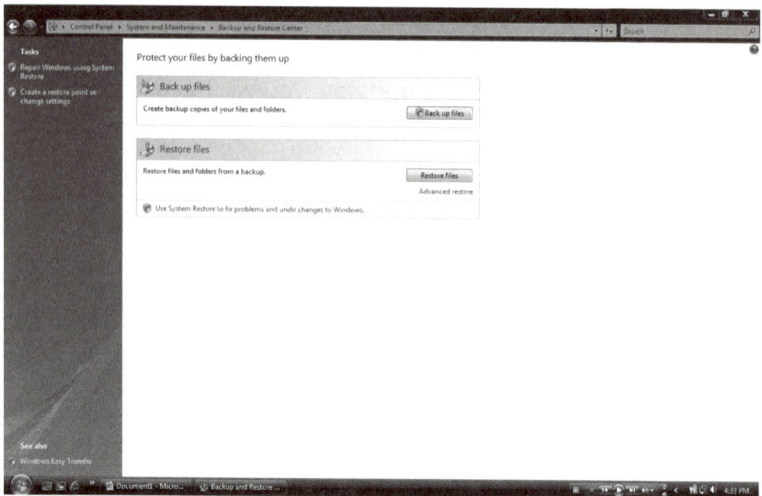

Figure 12.5
The Backup and Restore Center is where you can create system restore points.

System Restore is set to automatically create restore points for your computer. If, however, you are planning to install new hardware or software or make changes to some of the configurations, you can manually create a restore point that will bring you back to the state of the computer immediately before the install. To create a restore point, follow these steps.

1 Go to **Start > Control Panel**.

2 Select the **System and Maintenance icon** on the **control panel** to open the **System and Maintenance dialogue box**.

3 Select **Backup and Restore Center** to open the **backup and restore dialogue box** shown in Figure 12.5.

4 On the left side of the dialogue box, select **Create a restore point or change settings**. The **System Properties dialogue box** appears, as shown in Figure 12.6.

5 Select the **Create button**, near the bottom right corner of the dialogue box. This opens a **System Protection dialogue box**.

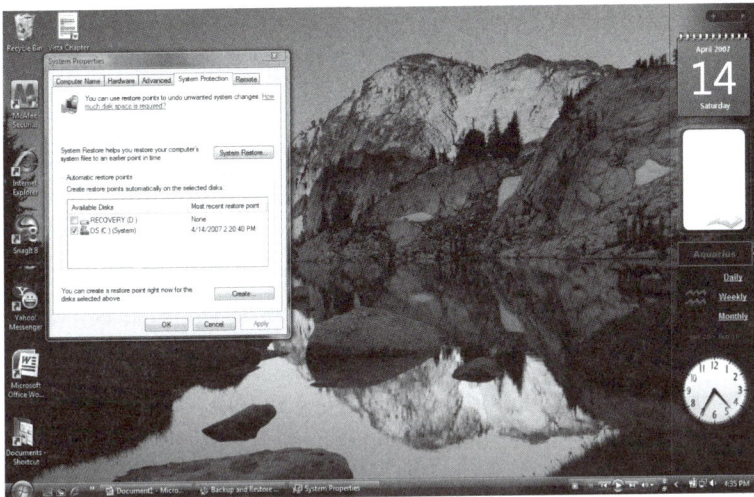

Figure 12.6
Use the System Properties dialogue box to create a restore point.

6 In the text box provided, type a brief description of the
restore point that you are creating. You can use any
description you like, but a date usually works best. When
you've finished, click by **Create.**

7 The computer will now begin to create your restore point.
This could take a little while, so be patient. When it has done
so, a confirmation message is displayed to let you know that
the restore point has been successfully created. Click on **OK**
to return to the **System Properties dialogue box**.

8 Click on **OK** to close the **System Properties dialogue box**,
then close the **control panel**. Your system restore point has
been set.

Restoring Your Computer to a Previous State

Once you have set a restore point, you can restore your
computer back to that state in the future if you need to. There
are two ways to do this, depending on whether you can boot
Windows or not.

Here is one way to restore your computer to a restore point.

1 If you can boot Windows, go to **Start > All Programs > Accessories**.

2 From the **Accessories** menu, select **System Tools** and then click on **System Restore**. The first screen of the **System Restore dialogue box** is informational. Read through the information and click on **Next.**

3 As shown in Figure 12.7, you need to choose the restore point you would like your computer to return to and then click on **Next**.

4 You are prompted to confirm your actions. If you're certain that this is the action you would like to take, click on **Finish**. This activates the restoration process.

5 To complete the process, restart your computer. Once the computer has rebooted, it should be as it was on the date of the chosen restore point.

If you cannot boot Windows, turn on your computer and hold down the **F8 key** until you see the **Startup Menu**. Select **Safe Mode** and press **ENTER** on your keyboard. This boots Windows into safe mode. You can then use the System Restore steps described above.

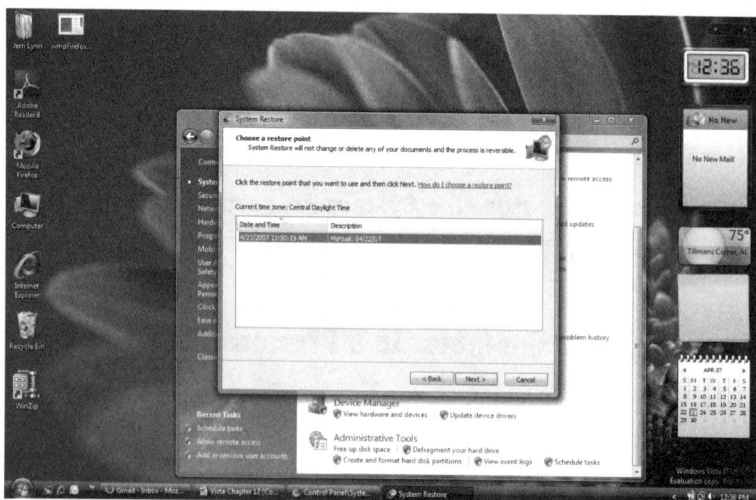

Figure 12.7
Select the Restore Point which you want your computer to return to.

→ Defragmenting the Hard Drive

The RAM on your computer is where programs and information are stored. Think of it as lots of small boxes. Each program and file on your computer uses some of those boxes and they're all stacked neatly, new programs and files using new boxes.

Over time, as you use your computer – install and uninstall programs, create and delete files – some of those boxes become empty. They aren't used because there isn't enough room in the available boxes to hold all of the information you need. To make the most of the space you have available, you need to rearrange those boxes so that all of the full ones are together and all of the empty ones are together.

Jargon buster

Defragmenting your hard drive places all of the sectors of your hard drive that are full together and all of the sectors of your hard drive that are empty together.

12

Defragmenting your hard drive enables your programs to operate more efficiently and should be done at least once every quarter, but it's best if you do it every month.

To defragment your hard drive, follow these steps.

1 Go to **Start > All Programs > Accessories**.

2 Select **System Tools** and then select **Disk Defragmenter.** This opens the **Disk Defragmenter dialogue box**, shown in Figure 12.8.

3 In the dialogue box, you have the option to set a schedule for when your hard drive will be defragmented or you can opt to defragment your drive immediately.

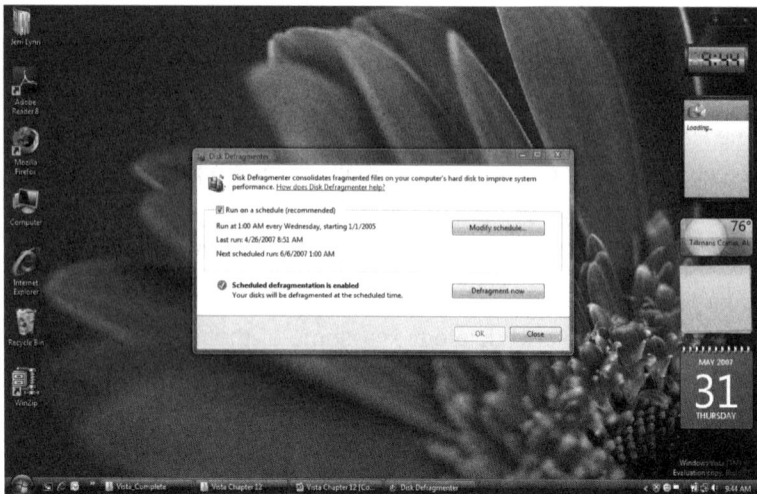

Figure 12.8
The Disk Defragmenter dialogue box gives you options for defragmenting your hard drive.

4 If you click on the **Defragment Now button**, the defragmenting of your hard drive will start.

Timesaver tip

Depending on how long it has been since the last time you defragmented your hard drive, it could take several hours for it to be completely defragmented and the process could slow down the performance of your computer during that time. For that reason, most people prefer to schedule defragmentation to occur during the late night hours when no one is using the computer. If you choose to schedule the defragmentation action of your hard drive, make sure that you leave the computer booted up on the appointed day.

5 When the defragmentation is finished, you are returned to the **Disk Defragmenter dialogue box**. Click on **Close.**

Just remember, if you schedule your defragmentation to happen at regular intervals, you shouldn't have to think about it in the future.

13

Improve Vista's Performance

In this lesson you'll learn how to get the best performance from Vista including how to tweak configuration, disable unnecessary features and change power settings.

Every new operating system claims to be better than the previous one. And most of them are. However, the default configuration of an operating system doesn't always optimise performance. This means you may have to make a few changes to get the best performance out of your operating systems – even Windows Vista.

Windows Vista performs really well right out of the box. It makes terrific use of system resources, but it's built for stability, security, and speed. Even so, there are some tweaks you can make to further improve the performance of Vista.

→ Vista Learns to Perform Better

One of the easiest ways to improve Windows Vista is to use it, because Vista builds on the Prefetch technology that was introduced in Windows XP. Prefetch was a method by which Windows XP could monitor and map your computer usage and then effectively anticipate that usage to improve speed and responsiveness.

Vista's improvement on Prefetch, called SuperFetch, also monitors your computer habits and caches the applications and processes that you use most often. However, SuperFetch anticipates more accurately what programs and processes you'll be using and keeps them ready. When you use these processes, it frees up virtual memory for other tasks but monitors your usage, learning more intimately the methods you use when computing.

When you're finished with a given application or process, the usage data is stored in a state of readiness for the next time that you use it. In other words, SuperFetch is in a constant state of adjustment, working to make your programs and processes as fast as possible.

If you use Vista regularly it only takes about a week for Vista to be fully optimised based on your usage habits.

→ Tweaking Configuration

When you install Windows Vista, all of the applications and processes are set to a default state. To help improve the performance of your computer, however, there are some minor configuration changes that you can make to improve speed and efficiency:

1 Select the **Start** button, right click **Computer** and then click **Properties**.

2 Select **Advanced System Settings**, as shown in Figure 13.1.

3 In the Performance section of the dialogue box, click **Settings**.

13

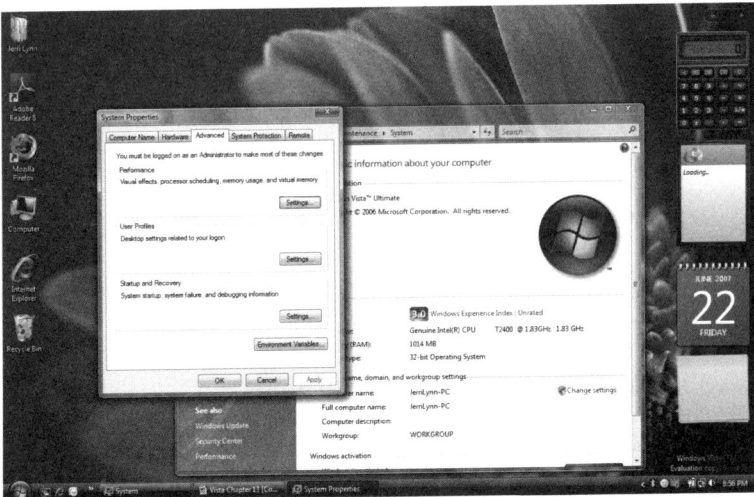

Figure 13.1
Use Advanced System Settings to change Vista's configuration.

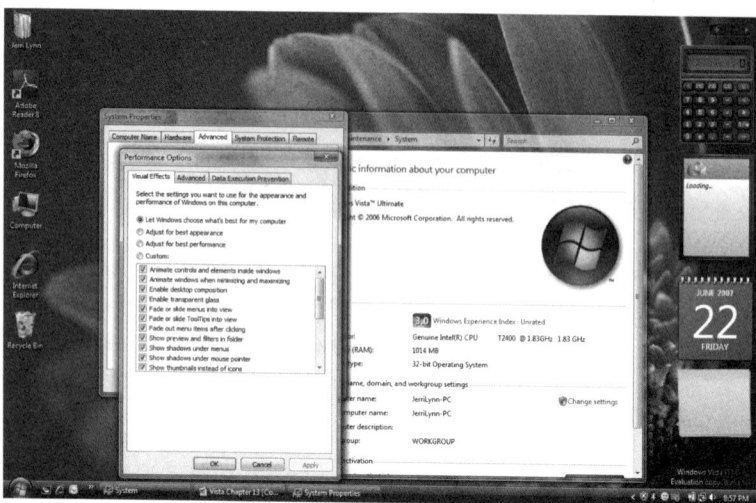

Figure 13.2
Change performance options in the Performance Settings dialogue box.

4 In the **Performance Settings** dialogue box shown in Figure 13.2, uncheck the following options:

- Fade or slide menus into view

- Fade or slide tooltips into view

- Fade out menu items after clicking

- Show shadows under menus

- Slide open combo boxes

- Slide taskbar buttons

- Use a background image for each folder type

Disable Automatic Windows Services

Vista, like many other operating systems, contains many services that automatically launch when your computer starts up. Disabling these services will speed up the performance and efficiency of your system.

To disable selected services:

1 Go to **Start > Control Panel** and select **System and Maintenance**.

2 Select **Administrative Tools** and the dialogue box shown in Figure 13.3 appears.

3 Select **System Configuration** and then click the **Services** tab, as shown in Figure 13.4. From the list that appears, disable the following services by removing the check mark next to each one:

■ Offline Files

■ Tablet PC Input Service

■ Terminal Services

■ Windows Search

■ Fax

4 Click **Apply** and then **OK** to close the dialogue box.

13

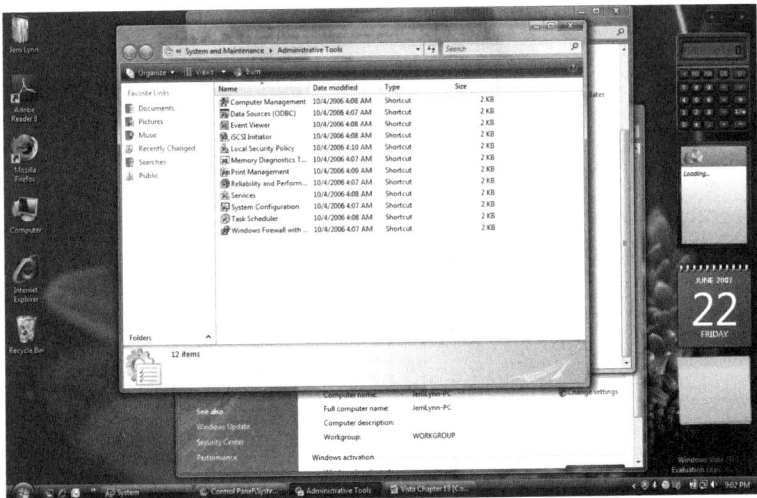

Figure 13.3
The Administrative Tools dialog box allows you to access System Configuration.

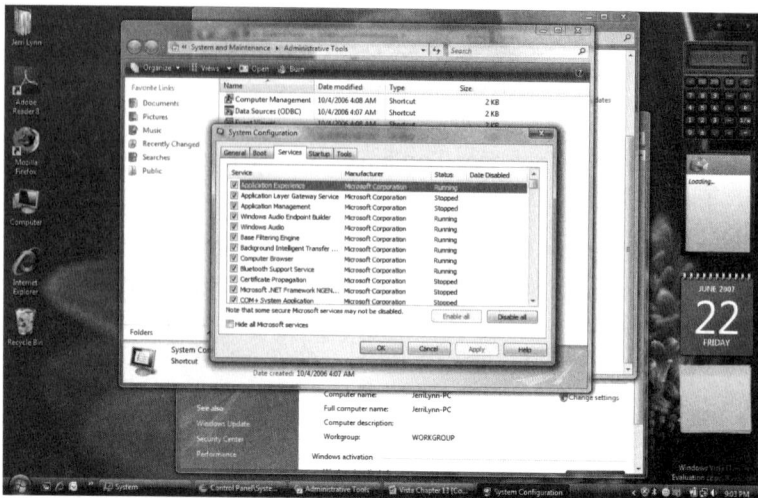

Figure 13.4
The Services tab gives you access to optional services.

> ## Important
>
> Each of the services listed above are optional. If you're using any of those services, then you should not disable them.

Disabling Unnecessary Vista Features

Startup services can slow your computer down considerably, but in addition to those features, there are several other options that you can disable that will also help to improve your speed and efficiency.

You can review and disable these features using these steps:

1 Go to **Start > Control Panel > Programs** and select **Program Features**, as shown in Figure 13.5.

2 From the menu on the left side of the dialogue box, select **Turn Windows Features on or off**. The **Windows Features** dialogue box shown in Figure 13.6 appears.

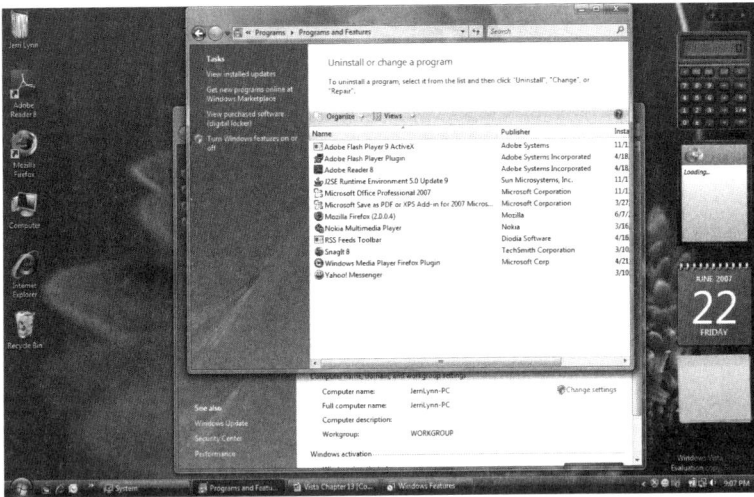

Figure 13.5
From the Program Features dialogue box you can turn Windows
features on or off.

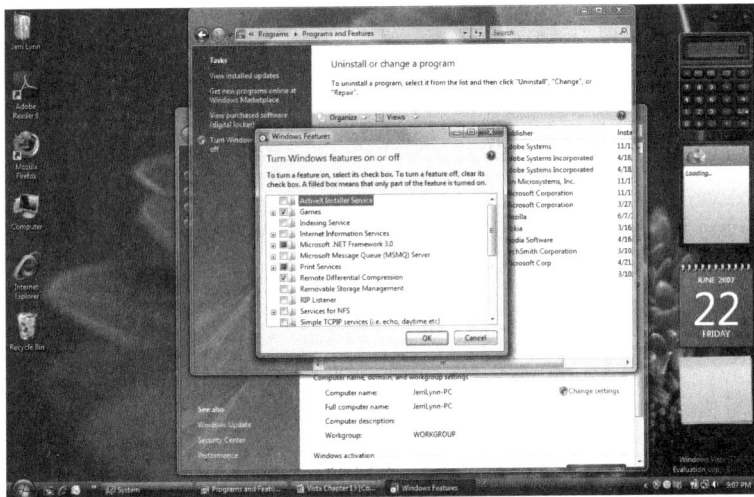

Figure 13.6
The Windows Features dialogue box.

3 Deselect the following options:

■ Indexing Service

■ Remote Differential Compression

- Tablet PC Optional Components

- Windows DFS Replication Service

- Windows Fax & Scan

- Windows Meeting Space

Timesaver tip

There may come a time when you need to re-enable these services. It's wise to create a list of the services that you're disabling in case you find that you need to restore one or more of them.

---

4 When you've finished making your selections, click **OK** to return to the **Programs and Features** dialogue box.

Speed Your Computer with Ready Boost

Windows Vista has a new feature that will come in handy if you're running low on memory in your computer. It's called Ready Boost, and the application will allow you to use a USB flash drive to enhance your computer's performance.

This features caches disk reads on the fly and can often speed up data access. However, you should not use Ready Boost as a replacement for memory upgrade, as it is a temporary solution.

To use Ready Boost follow these steps:

1 Insert a USB Flash Drive into your computer's USB port. The drive can be any size from 256 MB to 4 GB.

2 When the AutoPlay dialogue box shown in Figure 13.7 appears, select **Speed up my system**.

3 The system will automatically test the USB Flash drive to determine if it is compatible with the program and if it has enough space. If the USB Flash drive contains sufficient space, you'll be able to select whether to use it to speed up

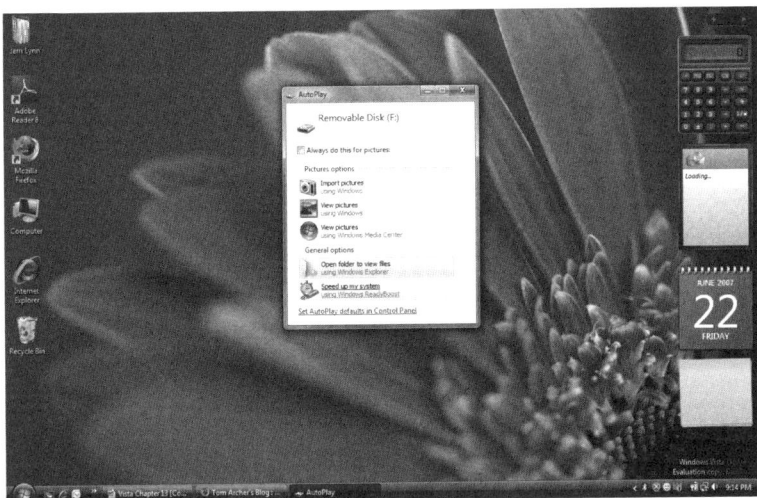

Figure 13.7
The AutoPlay dialogue box should appear when you plug in the Flash drive.

your computer and the amount of space you'd like to dedicate to the task.

4 If the USB Flash drive you're using is incompatible with the Ready Boost application, you'll receive a message like the one shown in Figure 13.8.

13

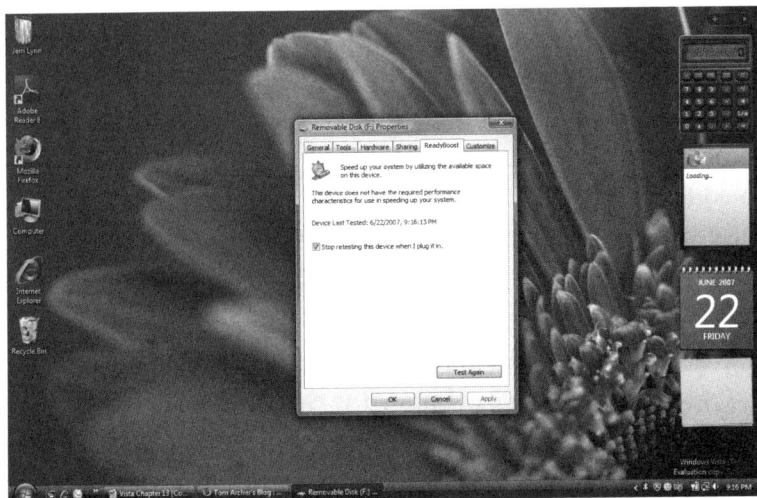

Figure 13.8
Not all USB Flash drives will work with the Ready Boost application.

5 When finished selecting settings, click **Apply** and then **OK** to close the dialogue box. The computer will then use the USB Flash drive as an external cache.

→ Change Vista's Power Settings

One nice feature of Windows Vista is that it has three different power settings to allow you to manage your computer's power according to your needs. This is an especially helpful feature if you're using a laptop computer. By default the power setting is the **Balanced** plan that limits the CPU to 50%. To change your power settings, use these steps:

1 Go to **Start > Control Panel > Systems & Maintenance > Power Options**.

2 In the **Power Options** dialogue box (shown in Figure 13.9) click the radio button next to **High Performance**. This increases the speed with which your computer processes commands.

→ Removing Even More Services

In addition to the services that you've already removed or disabled on your computer, there are myriad other services that you may not need. To find and disable more of those unnecessary services, take these steps:

1 Select the **Start** button and then type **services.msc** into the search box and press **Enter**. The **Services** dialogue box shown in Figure 13.10 appears.

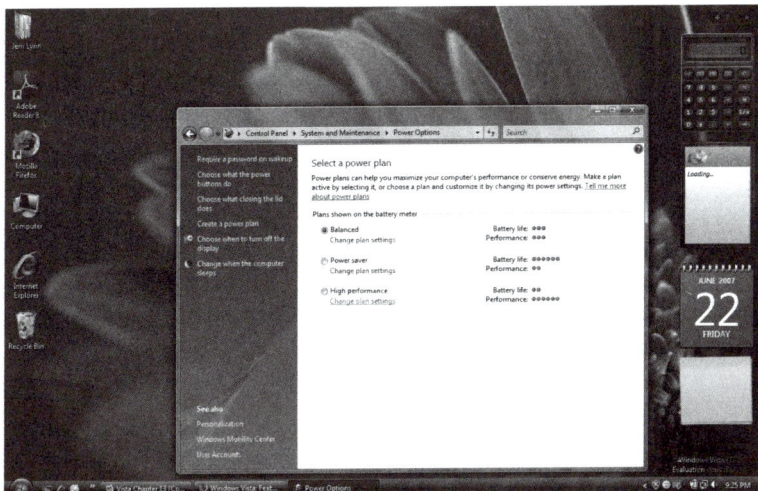

Figure 13.9
Manage your Power Options according to battery or performance need.

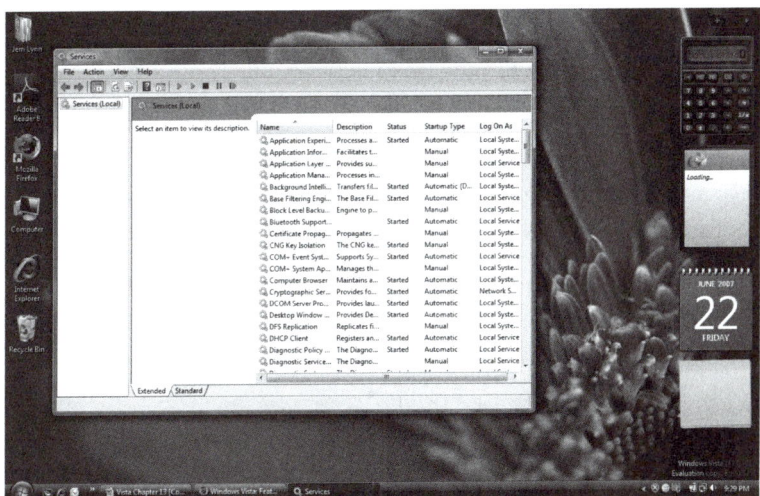

Figure 13.10
The Services dialogue box allows you to manage even more services on your computer.

2 In the dialogue box, disable the following services:

■ DFS Replication

■ Diagnostic Policy Service (change this service to "Manual.")

■ Distributed Link Tracking Client

■ IKE and AuthIP IPSec Keying Modules

■ IPSec Policy Agent

■ KtmRm for Distributed Transaction Coordinator

■ Offline Files

■ Ready Boost (if you're not using it)

■ Remote Registry

■ Table PC Input Service (if you're not using a Table PC)

■ Windows Error Reporting Service

■ Windows Search (if you don't use it)

3 In order to change how each service starts, right-click the service and select **Properties**. That opens the dialogue box shown in Figure 13.11.

4 If you don't want a service to load, stop the service by selecting the **Stop** option.

5 Then, pull down the Startup Type list and select **Manual** or **Disable**.

> ### Important
>
> If you're unsure about the function of a service, you can set it to **Manual** so that if something calls it, it should start up. Only select **Disable** if you know you won't need a service.

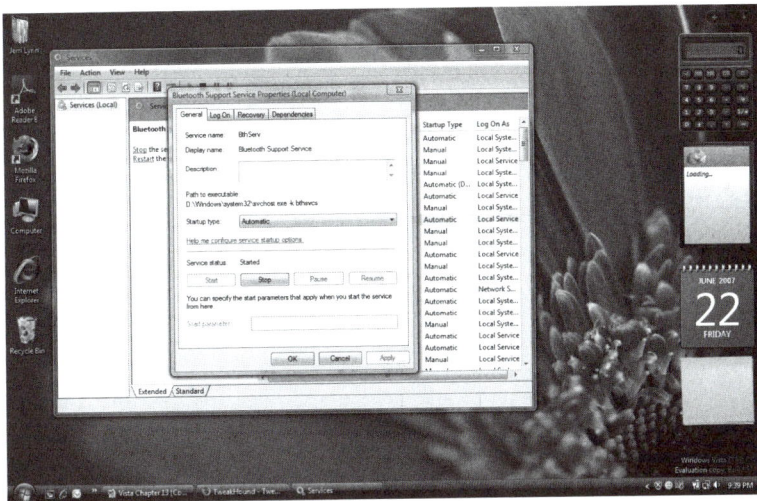

Figure 13.11
The Support Service Properties dialogue box.

The services you need depend on what you do with your PC. For instance, if you're not using Ready Boost, you can disable that service or you can disable Windows Error Reporting if you don't want to report errors.

Here are some of the services that you can disable:

- Computer Browser
- Distributed Link Tracking Client
- IKE and AuthIP IP Keying Modules
- Offline Files
- Remote Registry
- Tablet PC Input Service (unless you're using a tablet PC)
- Windows Error Reporting

→ Stopping and Removing Background Processes

Background processes are those processes that start as soon as you start your computer and run in the background all the time. These processes are indicated by the icons in the tray at the bottom or your screen, and they can seriously slow the performance of your computer.

To stop unnecessary processes from running follow these steps:

1 Go to **Start** and type **msconfig** into the search box. Press **Enter**.

2 The **System Configuration** dialogue box appears. Select the **Services** tab, as shown in Figure 13.12.

3 Deselect any unnecessary services that are running. What you consider necessary will vary from what others consider necessary because of your specific needs. Just make sure to make note of the services that you disable, in case you need to restore one of the settings.

4 Click **Apply** and then **OK**. It may be necessary for you to restart your computer before the changes take effect.

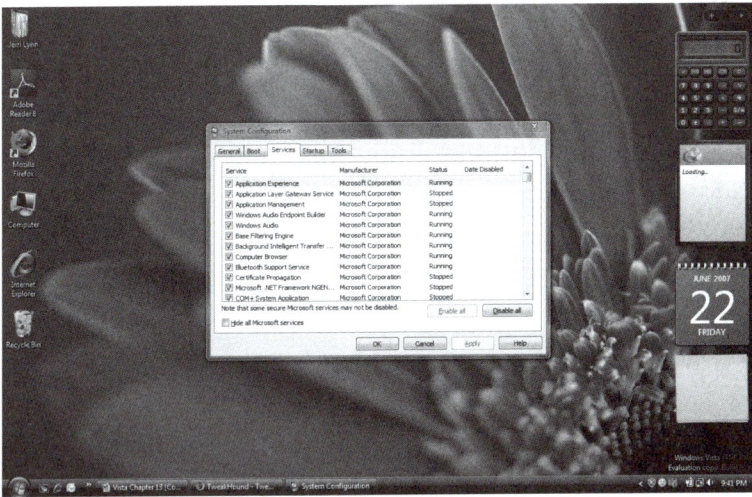

Figure 13.12
The Services tab on the System Configuration dialogue box lists
services that are running on your computer.

A general rule of thumb for removing services would be to look
for those third-party services that may exist on the list. These are
usually non-essential services unless they are related to security
applications.

In addition to the services that you have removed, there may be
startup applications – those applications that run automatically
on startup – that you can also remove to increase your
computer's performance.

Follow these steps to remove those startup applications:

1 Go to **Start** and type **msconfig** in the search box and press
Enter.

2 The **System Configuration** dialogue box appears. Click the
Startup tab, as shown in Figure 13.13.

3 In the list of startup programs shown on the **Startup** tab,
deselect the ones that you do not want to start automatically
when the computer starts. The rule of thumb for Startup
applications is that software applications should be okay to

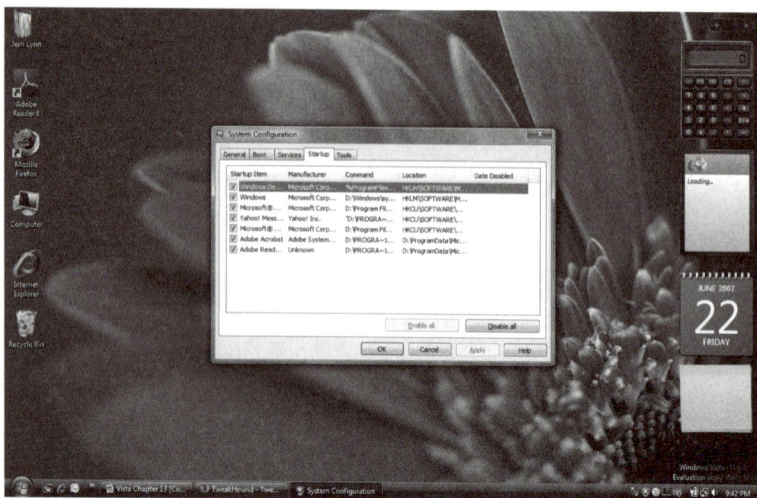

Figure 13.13
Deselect the Startup applications that you do not want to run automatically on startup.

disable unless they are security applications, but do not disable hardware applications.

4 When you've finished adjusting your startup applications, click **Apply** and then **OK**. You'll then need to restart your computer for the changes to take effect.

→ Increase Interface Performance

Along with Windows Vista came some very cool new interface capabilities. From the stylish transparencies of the windows to the cool animations and even the new sidebar, Vista is by far the most eye-catching new operating system we've seen in a very long time.

Unfortunately, even though it's very stylish, the new interface – called Aero – is a major drain on your resources. That means the operating system itself could bog down your computer if you're running Vista on a PC that's near or just above the system requirements.

It is possible to tweak the interface a bit to make it more resource friendly, however. It just takes a few little adjustments.

Disable Transparency

1 Right-click the desktop, click **Personalize**.

2 Select **Windows Color and Appearance**.

3 In the **Window Color and Appearance** dialogue box (shown in Figure 13.14), deselect **Enable Transparency**.

4 Click OK.

Remove Windows Sidebar

Windows Sidebar is a very cool new feature, but some of the gadgets included in the Sidebar can really eat away at your available resources. It's best to remove the sidebar if you're not using it:

1 Right-click the Sidebar and select **Properties**.

13

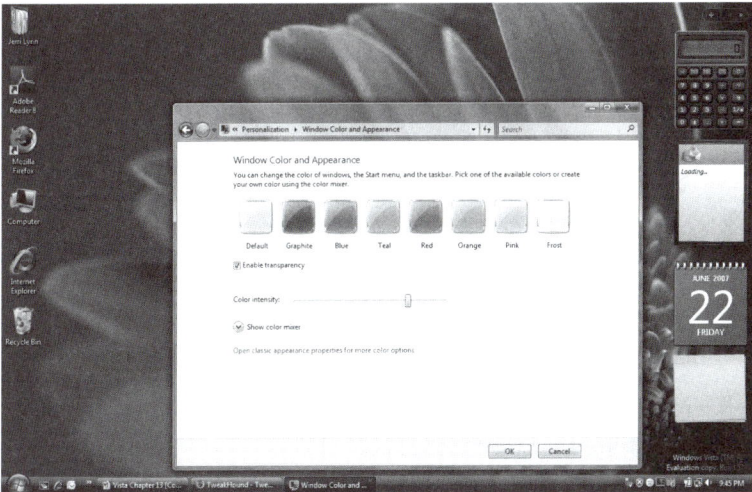

Figure 13.14
The Window Color and Appearance dialogue box allows you to adjust transparency settings.

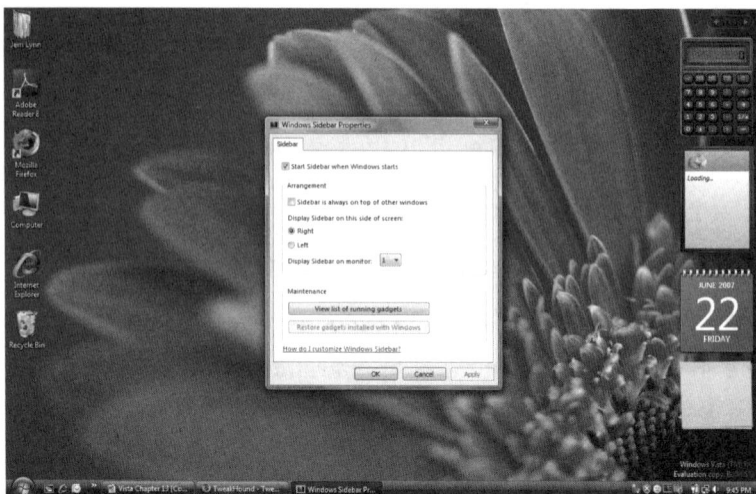

Figure 13.15
Control Windows Sidebar properties.

2 In the dialogue box that appears (shown in Figure 13.15), deselect **Start Sidebar When Windows Starts**.

3 Click OK and then right-click the Sidebar again.

4 Select Close Sidebar to disable it.

Adjust Visual Effects

Visual Effects can also be real resource hogs. To adjust Visual Effects, take these steps:

1 Go to **Start > Control Panel** and select **System and Maintenance**.

2 Select **Performance Information and Tools** and the dialogue box shown in Figure 13.16 appears.

3 From the menu on the left side of the dialogue box, select **Adjust Visual Effects**.

4 The **Performance Options** dialogue box appears, as shown in Figure 13.17. Deselect the effects that you don't find necessary or simply click **Adjust For Best Performance**.

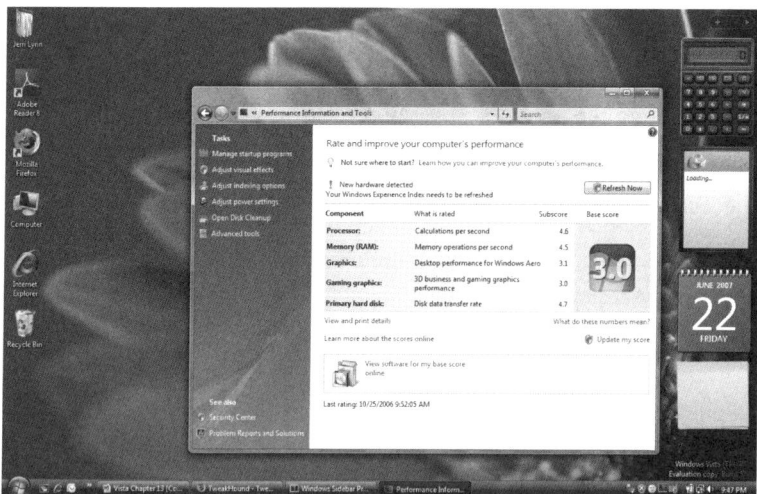

Figure 13.16
Use the Performance Information and Tools dialogue box to adjust
further settings.

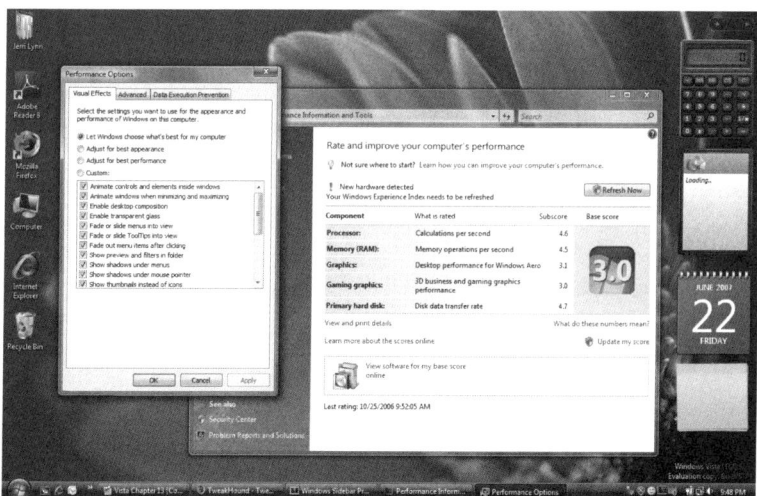

Figure 13.17
Use the Performance Options dialogue box to adjust visual effects.

Choose a Classic Theme

Because Aero is a very resource intensive interface, you may prefer to use a classic or standard Windows theme. Here's how to change your theme:

1 Right-click the desktop and select **Personalize**.

2 In the dialogue box that appears select **Open Classic Appearance Properties**.

3 The dialogue box shown in Figure 13.18 appears. Select a classic or standard theme and click OK.

→ Defrag Your Hard Drive

You may remember that defragmenting your hard drive means to compress data segments together to create additional free space on your computer. It may seem like a small task, but defragmenting your hard drive can free up a lot of space, thereby

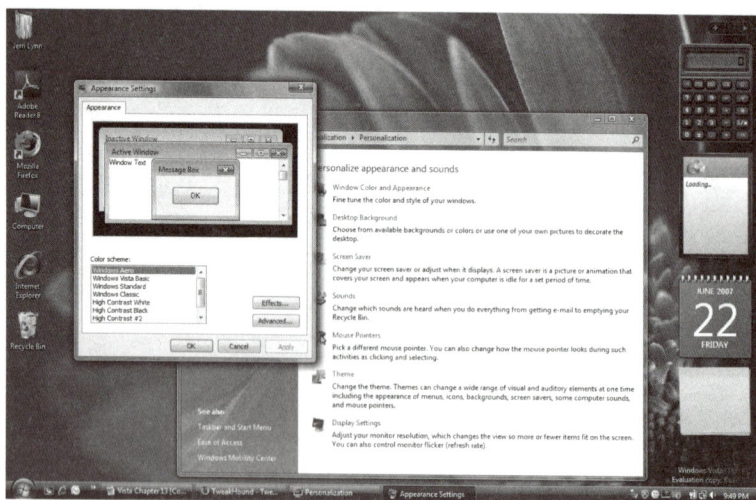

Figure 13.18
Use the Appearance dialogue box to adjust the theme for your computer.

increasing the efficiency and speed with which your computer performs.

Vista comes with a defragmenting program pre-installed. And the program is set by default to defrag your hard drive once a week. However, unless you keep your computer turned on all the time, that preset schedule might not work for you.

To change, or even disable the defragmenting schedule, follow these steps:

1 Go to **Start** and type in **defrag** in the search box. Press **Enter**.

2 The **Disk Defragmenter** dialogue box appears, as shown in Figure 13.19.

3 Use the controls in the dialogue box to reset or disable the scheduler.

4 When you've finished making your adjustments, click **OK** and then click **Close** to return to your desktop.

13

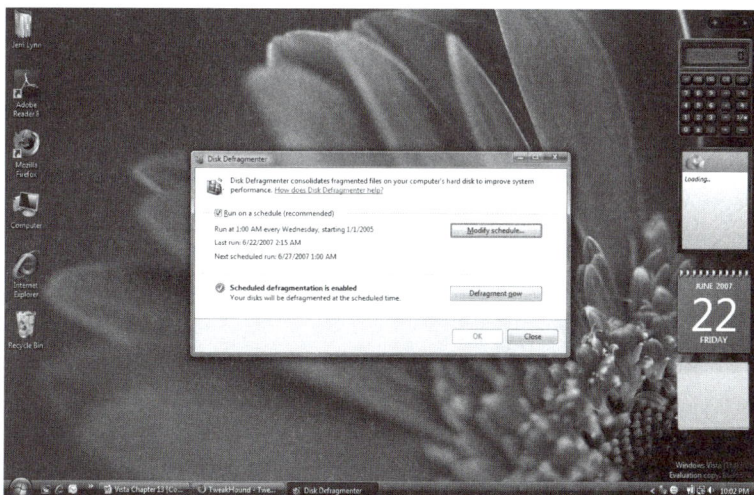

Figure 13.19
Use the Disk Defragmenter dialogue box to change a schedule or start a defrag.

Timesaver tip

Although the default setting for defragmenting your hard drive is one week, it's unlikely that you'll need to defrag that often. Unless you install and uninstall programs frequently, or move and delete data regularly, it's probably sufficient to defrag your hard drive about once a month. The defragmenting utility should be run at least once a month, however, to keep your system operating at optimum efficiency.

14

Troubleshooting Windows Vista

In this lesson you'll learn about troubleshooting Windows Vista, looking at software and driver issues, hardware, devices and printers.

Computers are complex machines that don't always work the way we expect them to work. If you have a problem with your Windows Vista machine, there are a few things you can do to solve that problem.

First, Vista will often recognise if there is a problem, and you don't have to do anything at all. If you encounter a situation where Vista recognises a problem and suggests a way to fix the problem, follow the prompts provided. You should be able to work through the issue as long as you're following the directions provided.

Another option for troubleshooting your Vista computer is to use the Help and Support dialogue box. You can access this dialogue box by selecting the Windows button and then choosing Help and Support. The Help and Support dialogue box appears, from which you can search for the solutions to whatever problem it is that you're experiencing. You can even search Windows Online or access other online help solutions if you don't find the answer to your problem.

There are some issues, however, that you can fix without going to the trouble of searching for the answers online. Those issues are addressed in the remaining pages of this chapter. You should be able to address each of these problems using the solutions provided without needing to access outside assistance.

→ Troubleshooting Windows Installation and Startup Problems

Q: I upgraded my PC to Vista Premium, but the installation didn't load very well so I decided to do a clean installation of Vista. Now when I enter the validation code, it says the code is in use. What's the problem?

A: Technically speaking, the validation code that you're entering is in use by you because you've already activated one copy of

Windows Vista with it. You should call the phone number listed in the installation wizard to receive a new validation code. The process takes only a few minutes and should be easy to work through. If the automated attendant is unable to get your copy of Vista activated, stay on the line and a live person will assist you.

Q: I just purchased Windows Vista Premium and went through the steps to upgrade my PC from Windows XP Professional. However, when I enter my product key I get a message that it is already in use or that it is invalid. What am I doing wrong?

A: Unfortunately, you cannot upgrade your operating system from Windows XP Professional to Windows Vista Premium. If you're using XP Professional, you should either upgrade to Windows Vista Business or Windows Vista Ultimate. Fortunately, you can still use the Vista version that you have by using the custom install method. Here's how:

1 Boot Windows Vista from the Installation Disk.

2 When prompted, **do not** enter the key code. Just click **Next** to continue with the setup. This will set up Vista as a 30 day trial.

14

3 When setup is complete, restart your computer to boot from the Installation Disk again. When prompted this time, enter the key code to activate your installation.

What you're doing is effectively installing Windows Vista Premium, and then installing it again on top of that installation. This circumvents the issue of upgrading from XP Professional to Vista Premium.

Q: Can I uninstall Windows Vista?

A: No. What you can do is reinstall your previous operating system, which will replace Windows Vista. You'll need your original installation disk to reinstall your old operating system. To regain the hard drive space used by Windows Vista, reformat the disk during the reinstallation process.

Q: I get the message "cannot copy files" during installation. What's wrong?

A: There are a number of problems that might cause you to get this message. Some possible causes for this problem include:

- Your Windows installation disk is scratched, smudged, or dirty. Clean the disk with a soft cloth, and then begin the Windows installation again. If the problem occurs again, your installation disk may be damaged and you may need to replace it.

- Your CD or DVD drive is not working properly, or the disk might be vibrating too much for the laser to accurately read the data.

- If your computer has multiple CD or DVD drives, it may be trying to locate files on the wrong drive. If your computer has a feature that allows you to disable CD or DVD drives that are not being used, use to disable the drives that you aren't using. Otherwise, try inserting the disk into a different drive, and then start the installation process again.

- There could be a virus on your computer. Scan your system to identify needed repairs and then disable the antivirus program and begin the installation process again.

Q: Why does my computer stop during installation and display a black or blue screen?

A: This is usually caused by hardware or software that is incompatible with Windows Vista. If you have this problem, try these suggestions:

- Uninstall or disable all antivirus software and restart your computer.

- If the installation fails again, there could be a hardware incompatibility problem. Check your hardware compatibility.

- If your hardware is compatible but your computer still stops responding, disable any unnecessary hardware; remove all

USB devices; remove or disable network adapters, sound cards, and serial cards; and then restart the installation.

Q: An error message appeared during installation. What do I do?

A: If you see an error message during installation, read it carefully and follow any instructions it contains to help you resolve the problem. If you need more information, go to http://www.support.microsoft.com and search for "**error messages when upgrading to Windows Vista**."

Timesaver tip

It's best to ensure that your computer is completely up-to-date before beginning the installation process. Updates that may be necessary (and could affect the installation process) include security and hardware driver updates.

Q: What do I do if my computer loses power while I'm installing Windows Vista?

A: If your computer loses power during installation, Windows attempts to return to your previous operating system. Before you try to install Windows again, eliminate the problem that caused your computer to lose power. Some of the issues that you may check include: power cables, power strips, and faulty parts.

After you have corrected the problem, try installing Windows Vista again.

Q: I can't find my product key. Now what?

A: If you don't have a product key to use during the installation process, you must buy a new one within 30 days after installation or Windows will stop working.

You can find your product key on your computer or on the installation disk holder inside the Windows package.

Q: I am getting a message that says my product key is invalid. What do I do?

A: There are a couple of reasons why a product key might not be valid:

- You mistyped the key.

- The key you typed does not match the key assigned to your copy of Windows.

First, try reentering your product key. If you receive the same error a second time, you may need to purchase a new product key. Call Microsoft's help system to receive the new key.

Q: I've installed Vista on more than one home computer, can I use the same product key on all of the computers?

A: You cannot use Vista on more computers than the Microsoft Software License Terms allow. Usually the license allows one copy of Windows to be installed on each computer. To use the same copy of Windows on another computer, you must first uninstall it on the first computer and then install it on the second one. After installing Vista, you'll need to reactivate the operating system, and you may need to call Microsoft to have your activation key reset.

→ Troubleshooting Software and Driver Issues

Q: Since I upgraded to Windows Vista, I have a program that is no longer working. What do I do?

A: First, try reinstalling the program. If that doesn't solve the problem you may need to purchase a newer version of the program – one that is designed to work with Windows Vista.

Q: Why can't I install a program made for an earlier version of Windows?

A: Most programs written for Windows XP also work in this version of Windows (Vista), but some older programs may run poorly or not at all. If an older program won't run correctly or doesn't install, start the Program Compatibility Wizard, which simulates an earlier version of Windows. You can run the wizard on the setup program itself if the program doesn't install, or you can run the wizard on the program if it installs but doesn't run correctly. You can access the Program Compatibility Wizard, shown in Figure 14.1, by going to **Start > Control Panel > Programs** and then clicking **Use an older program with this version of Windows**.

Q: I am an administrator on the computer, but a program I'm trying to install says I must have Administrator rights. What do I do?

A: If you are trying to install a program and you receive a message that you need to have Administrator rights, right-click the installation icon for the program, and select **Run as administrator**, as shown in Figure 14.2. You may be prompted to provide an administrator password.

14

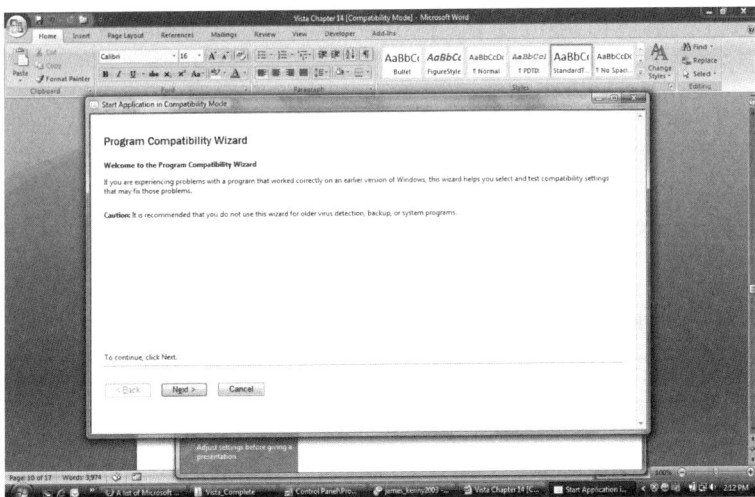

Figure 14.1
The Program Compatibility Wizard helps you run older programs on the Vista operating system.

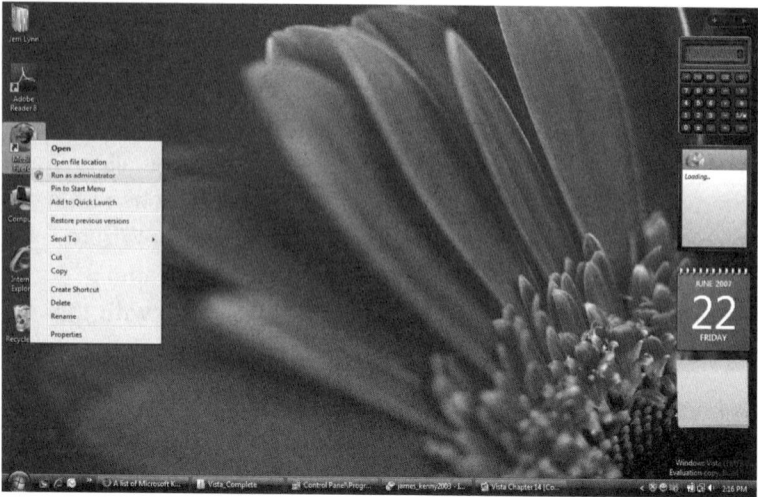

Figure 14.2
Right-click a program icon to run as an administrator.

If the program installs but does not run, right-click the program icon, click **Properties,** click the **Compatibility** tab, select the **Run this program as an administrator** check box, and then try to run the program.

Q: I'm trying to install a program directly from the Internet, but it won't install. What can I do?

A: If you can't install a program directly from the Internet, download the program's installation file and save it to your hard drive. Then, install the file from your computer, rather than from the Internet.

Q: I don't want a program to install to the default location. How do I change it?

A: You can usually install a program file in any location that you choose by selecting the location during the installation process.

Q: I installed a program but I can't find it in **Programs and Features**. Why is it not there?

A: Only programs that are compatible with Windows Vista appear in **Programs and Features**. If you don't see the program listed you should uninstall the program by going to **Control Panel > Programs > Programs and Features** and selecting **Uninstall a program**, as shown in Figure 14.3. Alternatively, some programs include an uninstall feature, which you can access from the **C:\Program Files** folder.

Q: I'm trying to install a program from CD, but the CD doesn't start automatically. What should I do?

A: If the program does not begin installing automatically, browse to the CD, go to the program's setup file (usually called Setup.exe or Install.exe), and double-click the icon to start the installation. If you try to browse the CD and cannot access it, there may be a problem with the disk or with the disk drive.

Q: What should I do if a program won't uninstall?

A: If the program doesn't uninstall completely the first time you try to uninstall it, sometimes running the uninstall program a second time will succeed.

If that doesn't work, try uninstalling the program while Windows is running in Safe mode.

14

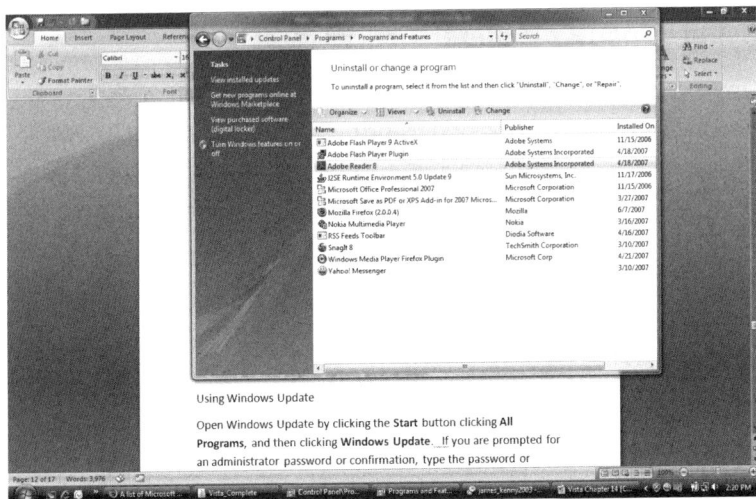

Figure 14.3
Use the control panel to uninstall unwanted programs.

> ### Timesaver tip
>
> If you installed a program recently and you want to uninstall it, you can try using the System Restore feature to return to the state it was in before you installed the program.

Q: What does it mean to **Change a Program**?

A: Some programs that appear in Programs and Features can, be installed or uninstalled, but they can also changed or repaired. Changing a program could mean that you're adding features to the program from the disk, or changing the configuration of the program in some other way. By clicking **Change**, **Repair**, or **Change/Repair** (depending on the button displayed), you can install or uninstall optional features of the program. Not all programs use the **Change** buttons; many only offer **Uninstall**.

Q: I'm installing a game and I keep getting an error that my drivers need to be updated. How do I update my drivers?

A: There are two ways to update your drivers:

Using Windows Update

Open Windows Update by clicking the **Start** button, selecting **All Programs**, and then clicking **Windows Update**. The Windows Update dialogue box, shown in Figure 14.4 appears. From there, you can check for and install updates. You may be prompted for an administrator password or confirmation.

To check for updates, click **Check for updates** in the menu on the left side of the dialogue box.

To see if updated drivers are available, click **View available updates**. Windows Update will list any updated drivers that are available for devices installed in your computer.

If updates are available, click the driver that you want to install, and then click **Install,** and follow the onscreen instructions.

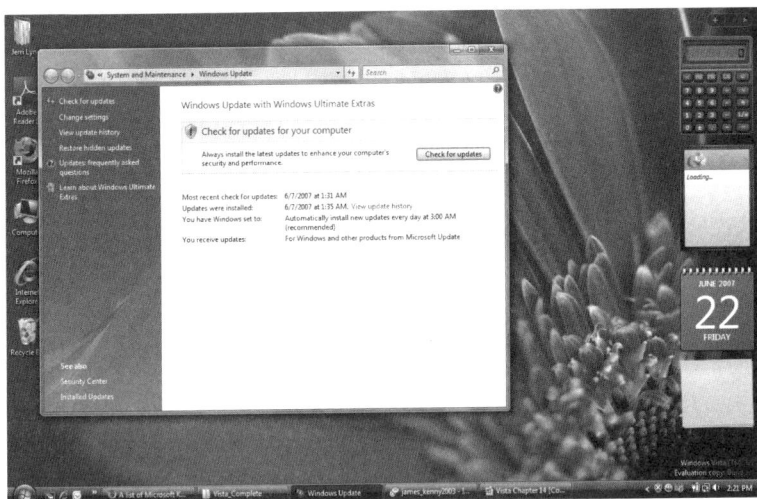

Figure 14.4
Use the Windows Update dialogue box to manage your updates.

Manually Update Drivers

To manually update drivers: Open Device Manager by going to
Start > Control Panel > System and Maintenance, and
selecting **Device Manager** (shown in Figure 14.5). You may be
prompted to enter an administrator password or confirmation.

In Device Manager, locate the device you want to update, and
then double-click the device name. In the **Properties** dialogue
box that appears (shown in Figure 14.6), click the **Driver** tab, and
then select **Update Driver**.

→ Troubleshooting Hardware, Devices and Printers

Q: I can't find hardware listed in my device manager that should
be there. What can I do?

A: If you cannot find the hardware you expect to find, it is likely
the hardware is installed incorrectly. You turn off your computer

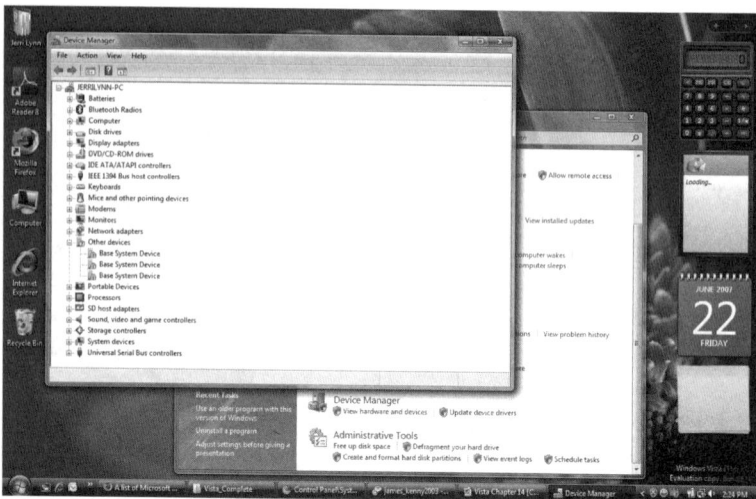

Figure 14.5
Use the Device Manager to manually update drivers.

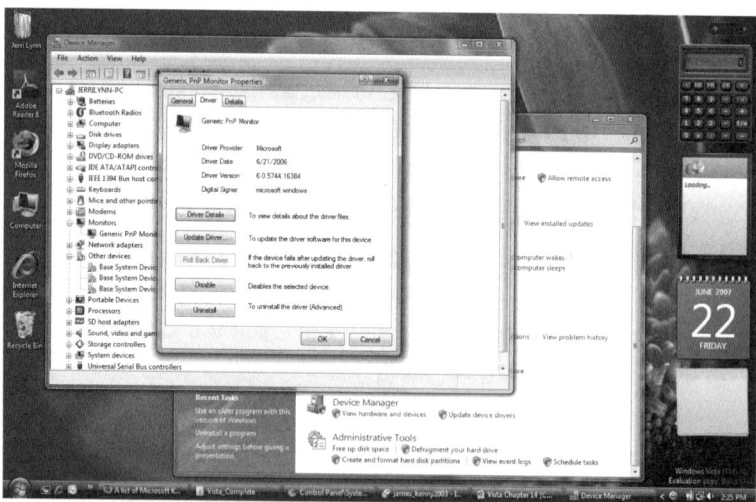

Figure 14.6
Use the Properties dialogue box to update device drivers.

and verify that the hardware is installed correctly. When you're sure it is, restart your computer. If the hardware was previously installed incorrectly, when the computer reboots, Windows should automatically detect the hardware and begin the installation process. You may be asked to provide drivers during this installation.

If your hardware is installed correctly but still doesn't appear in Device Manager, the hardware may be faulty, and it's likely that you'll have to consult with the device manufacturer or a repair specialist.

Q: I have installed a device, but it's not working properly. What should I do?

A: If you're viewing your installed hardware in the Device Manager, a yellow exclamation mark next to your hardware, as shown in Figure 14.7, means the device is recognised by Windows but is not working properly. This usually indicates a driver problem. Update your drivers by following these directions:

1 From the Device Manager, right-click the hardware that's not working properly and select **Properties**.

2 Select the **Driver** tab.

3 Select **Update Driver**.

14

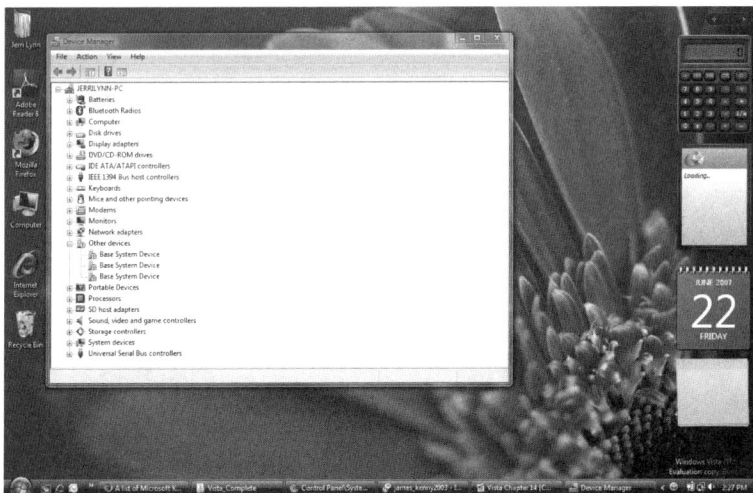

Figure 14.7
Viewing installed hardware in the Device Manager.

4 Then choose the options to **Search automatically for updated driver software**.

5 Windows automatically looks for updated drivers for your hardware. If Windows can't find updates, then you will need to manually download new drivers from the manufacturer's web site.

Q: The printer I want to install isn't recognised by the Add Print Wizard. How can I install it?

A: If Windows can't detect a printer that's connected to your computer, follow these steps to find and add the printer manually:

1 Go to **Start > Control Panel > Hardware and Sound**, and then select **Printers**. The **Printers** dialogue box, shown in Figure 14.8 appears.

2 Select **Add a Printer,** and the **Add Printer Wizard** appears.

3 In the **Add Printer Wizard**, select **Add a network, wireless or Bluetooth printer**, as shown in Figure 14.9.

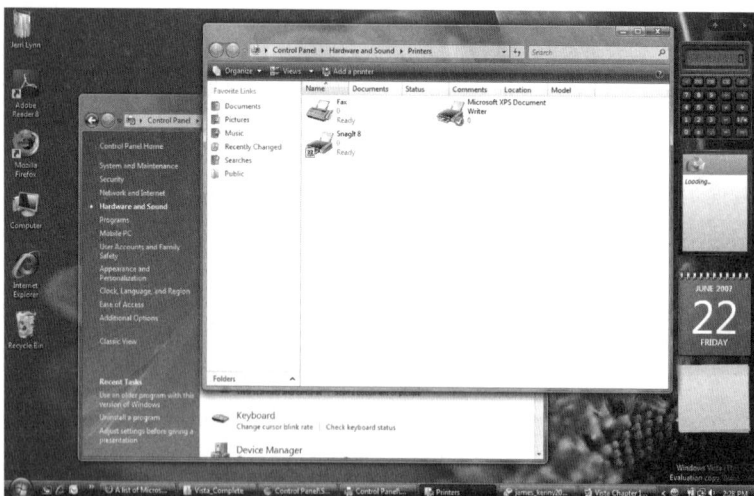

Figure 14.8
Use the Printers dialogue box to add new printers to your configuration.

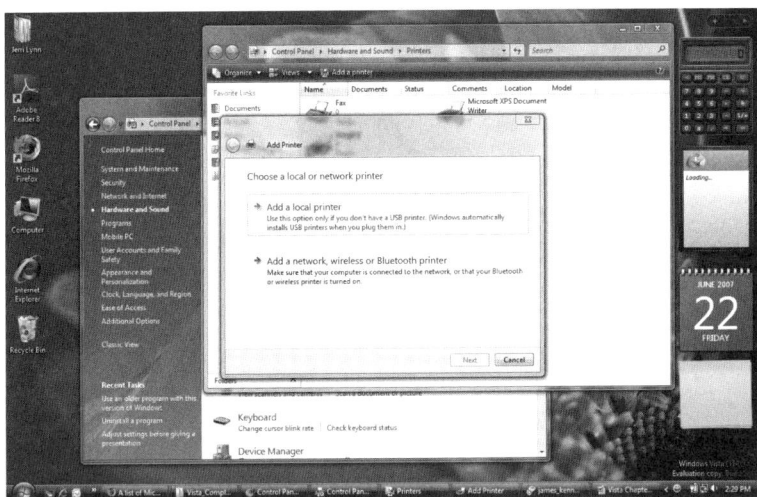

Figure 14.9
Add a printer to your network.

4 On the **Choose a network printer** page, click **The printer that I want isn't listed**.

5 On the **Find a printer by name or TCP/IP address** page, select how to find the printer that you want to use, based on the type or location of the printer (shown in Figure 14.10) and then click **Next**.

6 Complete the additional steps provided by the wizard, and then click **Finish**.

Q: How do I check the status of a USB device that I have connect to my computer?

A: To check the status of a device that's connected to your computer, you must be logged on as an administrator. Once you're logged in, take these steps to check device status:

1 Go to **Start > Control Panel > System and Maintenance**, and select **Device Manager**. You may be prompted for an administrator password or confirmation.

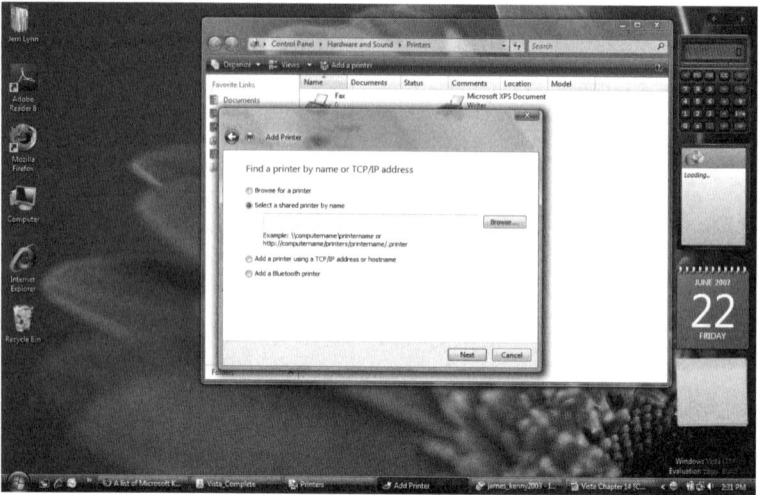

Figure 14.10
Tell the wizard how to find the printer that you want to use.

2 Locate the appropriate device category and double click it to expand the devices within the category.

3 Locate and right-click the entry for your USB device. As shown in Figure 14.11, a pop-up menu appears.

4 Select **Properties** to open the **Properties** dialogue box.

5 Click the **General** tab, and then look in the **Device status** box (shown in Figure 14.12) to see if any problems are displayed.

6 When finished, click **OK** to return to the **Device Manager**.

Q: How do I keep devices from using the AutoPlay feature each time I plug them into my computer?

A: Open AutoPlay by going to **Start > Control Panel > Hardware and Sound**, and then selecting **AutoPlay**. As shown in Figure 14.13, the **AutoPlay** dialogue box opens.

To never see the AutoPlay dialogue box, select **Take no action** next to the device or disk. To choose an action each time you

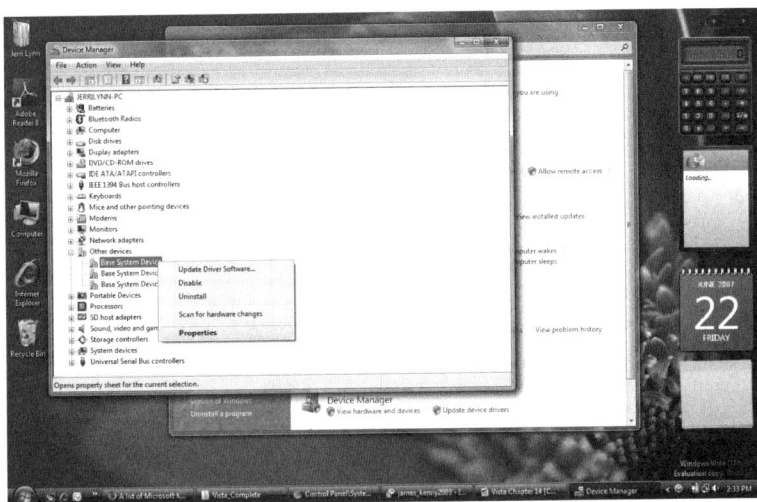

Figure 14.11
Right-click a device for an additional menu of possible actions.

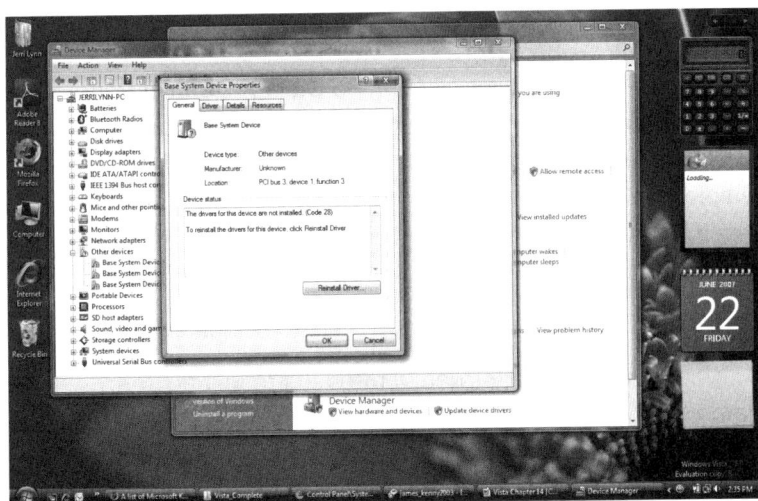

Figure 14.12
The Device status box lists device problems if there are any.

plug in a device or insert a disk, select **Ask me every time**. To have a program open automatically each time, select that program.

Q: How do I find out what kind of video card my computer has?

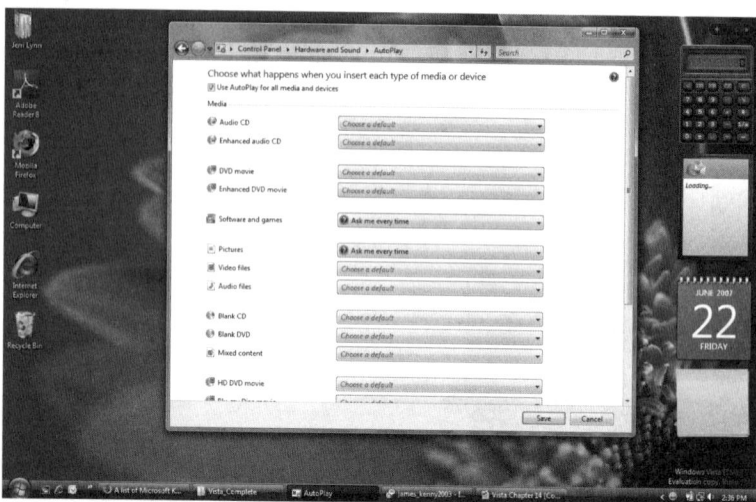

Figure 14.13
Use the AutoPlay dialogue box to choose how AutoPlay devices behave.

A: Open Display Settings by going to **Start > Control Panel > Appearance and Personalization > Personalization**, and then selecting **Display Settings**. As shown in Figure 14.14, the **Display Settings** dialogue box appears. The type of video card that's in your computer should be listed just below the monitor display.

Q: Why will my monitor only show limited resolution?

A: When Windows is installed, it attempts to identify the hardware in your computer. If it doesn't recognise the video card in your computer, by default, Windows will install a generic video driver. This generic driver usually does not provide the same level of support as a driver written specifically for the video card.

To fix this problem, you need to install the correct driver for your video card. Go to your video card manufacturer's website to download a driver. You'll need to know the make and model of your video card.

Q: I can't hear sound from my computer. What can I do?

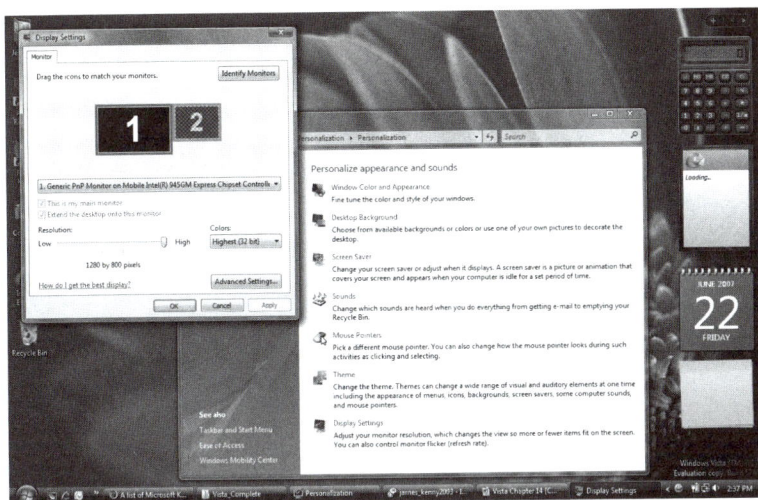

Figure 14.14
The Display Settings dialogue box.

A: Open the **Device Manager** and expand the **Sound, video and game controllers** category. If a sound card is listed, you have one installed. If no sound card is listed, you'll need to have one installed.

14

!

Important

If you know you have a sound card installed but it's not listed in the **Sound, video and game controllers** category, expand the **Other devices** category and check the devices listed there. Sometimes, Windows will install devices in this category because it doesn't recognise what category the device should be listed under.

If the device is listed, you'll know there's a problem if there is a yellow question mark next to the name of the sound card.

To identify the problem, right-click the name of the sound card, and select **Properties**. Click the **General** tab, and then look in the **Device status** box to see an explanation of the problem.

brilliant
pocket books

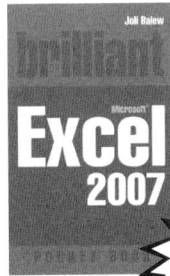

brilliant Joli Balew
Office 2007
POCKET BOOK

brilliant Joli Balew
Word 2007
POCKET BOOK

brilliant Joli Balew
Access 2007
POCKET BOOK

brilliant Joli Balew
Windows Vista
POCKET BOOK

brilliant Joli Balew
PowerPoint 2007
POCKET BOOK

brilliant Joli Balew
Outlook 2007
POCKET BOOK

brilliant Joli Balew
Excel 2007
POCKET BOOK

ONLY £8.99

The ultimate pocket sized guides to the new Windows Vista and Office 2007

brilliant pocket books – the fast answer